IN PU[RSUIT]
OF WHO[LENESS]

Healing in Today's Church

Bernard Häring, C.SS.R.

LIGUORI
PUBLICATIONS

One Liguori Drive
Liguori, Missouri 63057
(314) 464-2500

Imprimi Potest:
John F. Dowd, C.SS.R.
Provincial, St. Louis Province
Redemptorist Fathers

Imprimatur:
+ Edward J. O'Donnell
Vicar General, Archdiocese of St. Louis

ISBN 0-89243-236-5
Library of Congress Catalog Card Number: 85-80000

ACKNOWLEDGMENT

My heartfelt thanks go to Mrs. Josephine Ryan who, with her usual generosity and care, polished my English and typed this text, and to her friend Miss Marion McCracken who checked the typescript.

TABLE OF CONTENTS

INTRODUCTION

On the occasion of the beatification of the Redemptorist Peter Donders (May 23, 1982), the faculty of missiology at the Gregorian University (Rome) decided to establish a chair which would promote a closer union between sharing the Good News and the ministry of healing. I am most grateful to the University for inviting and urging me to initiate this new chair; for it gives me the opportunity to concentrate my study and reflection on this important area which, in my opinion, theology has neglected for a long time.

It gives me great pleasure to honor in this way our blessed confrere, Peter Donders, who, by his long priestly life as apostle to the lepers, actually lived this perfect blend of sharing the Good News and caring for the sick. He freely chose to go where human misery cried most pitifully for help. There, in Surinam, among the poorest of the poor, he felt closer to his Savior and divine-human Healer.

The following pages have been written to answer the question: What does humanity need the most in today's world? What is needed is a systematic integration of the message of salvation and the *diakonia* (service) for people's health — an integration that creates a whole and healthy relationship on all levels and in all personal and community areas.

Such fundamental reflections require a careful diagnosis with the following questions in mind: What are the main causes and what are the chief symptoms of the greatest evils and most damaging illnesses afflicting humankind today? Where can we find the most hope-inspiring healing forces? What is the present condition of the healing professions and the prevailing models of health care? How does the Church envision her mission in this field? Does she realize the need and possibility of a new orientation inspired by the Gospel itself and by the present situation? Is she willing to embrace this new wholistic blend of sharing the Good News and healing the sick, in faithfulness to the example and mandate of the Lord?

James McGilvray, speaker for an ecumenical commission which has studied this theme during the past decade, writes in *The Quest for Health and Wholeness:* "The Church, which is the organized and visible expression of Christian discipleship, has always had some difficulty in discovering how it should respond to its Lord's command to heal. In contrast to the other imperatives — to preach, teach and baptize, whose implementation has presented no problems — the imperative to heal has always created some confusion."

It seems that one reason for this difficulty was and is that theology did not successfully incorporate the *diakonia* for the sick as an integral part of her total mission. It did not understand how intimately and inseparably interwoven are the kerygma of salvation and the healing ministry to sick people, as well as to sick cultures and societies. That they belong together is evident from the core of New Testament tradition about the mission of the apostles, the disciples, and the whole community of disciples.

Luke, the physician and evangelist, speaks of the mandate to heal that was given not only to the twelve apostles but also to seventy-two disciples. After having brought back to life the daughter of Jairus, Jesus ''called the Twelve together and gave them power and authority to overcome all the devils and to cure diseases, and sent them to proclaim the kingdom of God and to heal. . . . Everywhere they told the good news and healed the sick'' (Luke 9:1-6). When ''the Lord appointed a further seventy-two and sent them on ahead in pairs . . . '' he instructed them to ''heal the sick there, and say, 'The kingdom of God has come . . . ' '' (Luke 10:1,9).

The Gospel of Matthew is no less explicit about the mandate to heal the sick as an integral part of the mission of the twelve: '' . . . as you go proclaim the message: 'The kingdom of Heaven is upon you.' Heal the sick, raise the dead, cleanse lepers, cast out devils'' (Matthew 10:7-8). The closing part of Mark's Gospel clearly indicates the dimensions of the healing mandate, for there it is clear that all the believers are included: ''Faith will bring with it these miracles: believers will cast out devils in my name . . . and the sick on whom they lay their hands will recover'' (Mark 16:17-18). What this Gospel says very concisely about the infant Church — '' . . . the Lord worked with them and confirmed their words by the miracles that followed'' (Mark 16:20) — is exemplified in great detail by the Acts of the Apostles.

These pages will also discuss which are the evil spirits and devils to be driven out by the Church in fulfillment of her total message and, above all, which are the ailments and illnesses that the Church is entitled and obliged to heal in fulfillment of her salvific mission.

Chapter One

IN SEARCH
OF A UNIFIED WHOLENESS
AND HEALING

In our time, the scientific and technical development of medical science and practice is breathtaking. The battle against most of the traditional epidemics is highly effectual. Ever more effective medications are being discovered to combat viruses, bacilli, etc. Not less astonishing is the progress in surgery, making possible the transplant of hearts and many other organs. Thousands of patients in numerous intensive care units are brought successfully through dangerous crises. Even hearts that have stopped beating have been made to beat again.

In light of the questions proposed in our Introduction, how do we assess the value of this modern progress?

Evaluation of the modern technical
model of health care

The above-described development is attained at a very high price. The total expenses imposed by the present technical medical model are fantastic, comparable only to the cost of the senseless arms race. Moreover, the advantages of the costly "health industry" benefit only a relatively small minority of the world's population. And the enormous private and public spending on this sector lessens the funds, materials, and personnel that could be available for preventive medicine, health education, rehabilitation of handicapped persons, and effective care for the whole population.

According to recent surveys, these expensive medical techniques can be afforded by no more than ten to twenty percent of the population of the developing countries. While millions of people are unwell and crippled because of malnutrition and lack of medical care, enormous personal and material resources are spent on procedures that do not serve life and health at all but only prolong the process of dying. Serving no good purpose and benefiting no one, this is done, seemingly, only to show that it is technically possible — and maybe also to quiet the collective conscience of a pro-abortion society. Think of the proportion — or rather the disproportion — between expenditure for prolonging the death process and expenditure for care of children damaged by their environment or suffering from genetically acquired maladies.

Behind all these evident facts there are deeper problems. For vast parts of our population in the industrial countries, burgeoning health care has become an idol or, speaking in biblical terms, a demon that has to be driven out. Even the vocabulary is deceitful. We hear expressions like "health industry" and, worse, "health delivery" whereby health becomes one among the many things to be bought and sold. People claim a right to health care from the state, from welfare — to be delivered by some kind of high-priestly doctors — while at the same time gravely damaging their health by an insane life-style governed by insatiable appetites and/or by refusing to take proper care of their own and others' health. They give no thought to promoting a healthy environment and human milieu. Thus the health industry becomes a part of that way of life, that consumerism which increasingly disturbs the ecological equilibrium which is already terribly threatened by the industrial-military complex of the superpowers and their satellites.

Pestilential diseases are now under control in most parts of the world; but millions of people in some countries still suffer from leprosy and similar contagious diseases which could easily be conquered if there were more effort to engender human and Christian solidarity. Perhaps this incredible refusal to rescue people from these terrible diseases has much to do with the many destructive diseases afflicting the world of our rich and consumer society. We have "epidemics" of alcoholism, drug addiction, and many other ailments induced by lack of discipline, by spiritual emptiness, and by the stress of senseless competition. And this condition continues because people can rely on "health delivery" to cure the ravages of their self-inflicted diseases.

In the so-called "developed" nations, "former environmental deficiencies," according to J. McGilvray, "have been replaced by such unhealthy practices as industrial pollution and personal indulgence in drinking, smoking and over-eating. . . . Efforts to change life-styles which are injurious to health are tolerated, provided they do not bring into question the system which promotes their use under the guise of exercising personal freedom and choice. Hence, people are subjected constantly to the wiles of advertising that encourage them to want and consume more and more, including things injurious to their health." Senseless desires become needs, and life-styles tend to reflect this.

People buy many things that are injurious to their health. Then, instead of living a healthy life in healthy relationship with others, they attempt to buy back their health which is offered as a salable article by their consumer society. These disastrous consequences can be measured to some extent. Some researchers have challenged the present system even on the basis of cost analysis. They point to surveys which reveal that up to half of the people admitted to hospitals could have prevented the conditions that brought on their illnesses. Add to this statistic the numerous people who, for one reason or another, fail to come to our hospitals or are not reached by the present model of health delivery.

The point, surely, is not that those people who come with self-induced health problems should not be helped but, rather, that they should be helped effectively to prevent this suffering and/or to take up their own responsibilities, at least for the future. From whom, then, should we expect the most decisive moves: from the civic community or from the community of believers?

Sixty percent of deaths among today's American adults are caused by heart attacks, strokes, and cancer. A recent survey of the U.S. National Center for Health Statistics indicates that at least six of the leading causes of death "reflect the state of despair, physiological or emotional, into which our society has fallen. After heart disease, cancer and cerebrovascular disease, the fourth is accidents, the seventh cirrhosis of the liver, and suicide is ninth." Add to this the many man-made diseases which, while not fatal, make life miserable for their victims. Doctors tell us frankly: "It is our deliberately chosen and cultivated Western life-style — what we eat, drink and smoke — that causes most illness."

The prevailing scientific-technical medical model is so disproportionately busy repairing bodily disfunctions and defects that it becomes blind to the deeper cultural, societal, and spiritual situations that make so many people pitiably ill. In this situation we look to the findings of new anthropological schools of medicine, to the psychosomatic medicines, and to the insights of various schools of psychotherapy.

But, while it is encouraging to see that therapy is beginning to develop a wholistic vision of humankind, we must face the sad fact that the prevailing trends in clinical psychology indicate that not much progress has been made in this area. A. E. Bergin studied thirty leading textbooks on clinical psychology (psychotherapy) and found that they do not even mention "God" or the "spiritual dimensions" of human beings. While they claim to study and act on the basis of a "value-free" approach, they are far from being neutral; they are actually inimical to the wholistic vision which includes a theistic conviction. How, then, can they restore people to wholeness?

That these attitudes are erroneous can be seen from actual experience. It has been shown that Mormons in Utah have thirty percent less incidence of cancer than the rest of the population. Regular churchgoers in Washington County, Maryland, have forty percent less risk of arteriosclerotic heart diseases. These and many other observations lead outstanding doctors and many alert Christians to question the prevailing model of health care. They want to know whether its understanding of humanity includes the existence of a soul within the body. They are asking: What is the exact status of the healing profession within this technical-scientific model? Who holds the balance of power? What are the limits within which this model can still render service?

So much, then, for the state of modern health care. Now, what about the Church's healing ministry in today's world?

Critique of the Church's healing ministry

There can be no doubt that the Church makes a major contribution to human health. To a great extent it comes as an indirect but important consequence of reconciliation with God, with one-self, and with neighbor and from a basic training in responsibility and co-responsibility. But the Christian churches of today are beginning to ask themselves whether they have been actually fulfilling the divine mandate to heal the sick in complete harmony with the ministry of salvation and in view of urgent needs.

There are three points on which most will agree: (1) Our theology departments during the last generations have paid little or no attention to the Lord's mandate for the Church to heal the sick as essential part of her mission. (2) The manuals of moral theology and specific treatises on medical ethics accepted the advance of modern medicine as merely dealing with sick organs rather than with the sick person viewed wholistically. Therapy was for dam-aged organs rather than for the psychosomatic-spiritual health of the person. The underlying anthropology was more that of Des-cartes than of the Bible and the best wholistic anthropology of today. In other words, Catholic medical ethics did not ask the basic questions about the anthropology on which the modern technical medical model is built. It did not discern the "spirit of the era" and, therefore, was unable to read the "signs of the time." (3) The missionary and charitable spirit of the churches and missiology generously promoted institutes for medical missions and for mar-velous medical activity in the mission countries. What has been done in the service of the sick deserves unreserved admiration. But for too long now not enough study has been given to the meaning and the role of healing with which the Church has been mandated: to proclaim the message of salvation and to heal.

Today there is a growing awareness, especially within the World Council of Churches and within the faculties of missiology, that the healing ministry of the Church can be understood and faithfully fulfilled only within a biblical and anthropological blending of the ministry of salvation and the healing of the whole person or community. And this is so not only for the sake of effective healing but equally for the fulfillment of the proclamation and celebration of salvation.

It must be acknowledged that the Christian missions have done much for medical education and for the pressing needs of the poor in the mission areas. The numerous medical missionaries and other nurses who reach large numbers of families in their dispensaries deserve special mention here. Lately, there has been a healthy development of "community medicine" in at least some mission countries. But, by and large, these dedicated missionaries and lay helpers are working in hospitals and clinics. Already in 1910, the evangelical churches were supporting 2,100 hospitals and 4,000 clinics in mission countries. Gradually, the Catholic mission has reached the same level and even surpassed it.

Probably the chief weakness here is that the mission hospitals and clinics have generally followed the modern technical medical model. Because of the later explosive increases in the cost of this type of institution, even the poor had to pay in order to keep them functioning. Thus, hospitals originally erected for the poor began to serve the privileged class more than the very poor.

As far as the Protestant missions are concerned, James McGilvray notes that "95% of the churches' medical activities were focussed around curative services in hospitals and clinics. Very little was done to promote health or prevent disease." The Catholic mission does not show quite the same disproportion, at least not during the last decade.

The new approach, promoted by the World Council of Churches and also within the Catholic Church, focuses much more on preventive medicine and general health education. Much has been done, and more must still be done, to eliminate past overemphasis on specialization. The Church as a whole, and each community, has to be seen as and transformed into a "healing community."

Through the integrated ministry of the Church, people would come to know what truly human health means and how each person and each community can promote healthy, healing relationships and conditions of life. But we should also learn how to discover in illness and suffering a deeper meaning, and how to heal what can be healed and deal creatively with the rest. This, too, is part of truly human health in the light of redemption.

Hunger for wholeness and wholistic vision

The best thinkers on this subject have felt and still feel strongly that nothing is more needed for our sick people and our sick culture than "the spirit of wholeness." Their diagnosis for modern medicine is that it suffers from a "loss of wholeness," a "loss of the spiritual center."

One of the deep-seated causes of the crisis in modern medicine, and especially in the modern technical medical model, is a one-sided differentiation and specialization which, with almost unavoidable consequence, has blocked the vision of wholeness. "Differentiation is the cutting edge of the modernization process, sundering cruelly what tradition had joined. . . . Differentiation slices through ancient primordial ties and identities, leaving crisis and 'wholeness-hunger' in its wake." (So writes J. Murray Cuddihy in *The Ordeal of Civility*.)

In no area of human life is the loss of a wholistic vision so devastating as in the field of religion and health. The English word *health* comes from the same root, *hal*, as "whole" and "holy." The same affinity is found in the German *heil, heilig, heilen, heil sein* and the Latin word *salus* (health) is the root of *salvezza* (salvation) in Italian. Thus etymology itself indicates that salvation and health are interrelated and can be understood only when viewed wholistically. However, careful distinctions are needed here.

Modern medicine deals not only with a variety of functions but also with a variety of dimensions and levels. Surgery deals with physical functions and organs (at least primarily); medicative treatment works well on the level of chemistry; psychoanalysis and psychotherapy operate on the psychic level (self-awareness, perception, and so on); logotherapy gives special attention to the spiritual dimension. Social medicine and sociology of medicine emphasize human relationships, the interrelation of health and sickness with social processes, structures, and the like. There is sharp awareness of the interrelatedness of the sick person and the sick society, culture, and so on.

Since modern medicine developed in the context of modern science, and since scientific method developed it — adopting most of the uncontrolled and unconscious assumptions of modern natural sciences — it was almost natural for it to overlook the spiritual dimension of humanity or exclude it categorically. The consequences were the more disastrous because even the dimension of psychosomatic wholeness was being neglected or ignored. Experienced physicians finally came to realize that to ignore the spiritual dimension in this field is to cause harm to both patient and physician.

It is one of the positive signs of our time that more and more physicians and professors of medicine have begun to "hunger for wholeness." Many factors have contributed to this new development. Martin Marty remarks that medicine, once sure of its scientific future, is becoming more open to wholistic inquiry, thanks to pressure from patients, outside criticism, and second thoughts by medical and health professionals.

The same is true for many in the field of theology and missiology. There is a new awareness of the need for interdisciplinary research and reflection, based on a new wholistic vision which requires the cooperation of all concerned parties. As scientists and doctors begin to see more clearly that health and sickness cannot really be understood if the dimensions of salvation and wholeness are ignored, so, too, theologians have begun to realize that their striving for a wholistic vision is not adequate unless they integrate the insights of the various disciplines that study the human person and human life conditions.

However, these signs of progress should not make us overly optimistic. Because of the customary specialization and separation of the disciplines, it is still very difficult for many health professionals, as well as moralists, to arrive at wholistic vision and to adopt it in practice. Alexander Mitscherlich (in 1975) surmised that knowledge of psychology among doctors left much to be desired. The same author estimates that all somatic diseases are thoroughly or partially — either in their origin or their obstinancy — psychosomatically conditioned. Moral theology and pastoral formation have to give greater attention to this aspect.

During the last twenty-five years much new thought and many new beginnings have been taken in the whole field of healing, a swing to a wholistic approach within the churches and within the World Health Organization. There are promising initiatives of interdisciplinary research by various other groups. Worthy of mention are the ecumenical German Institute for Medical Missions, which cooperates with a qualified study group of the World Council of Churches; the Kennedy Institute for Bioethics at Georgetown University; and the Lutheran General Medical Center Foundation. There is also a new creative model of wholistic care for terminally ill persons called The Hospice Movement; this originated in England and is spreading also in the United States and other countries. Besides using the classical forms of treatment, this Movement places special emphasis on a beneficent human milieu, an atmosphere of acceptance and loving care on all sides.

Time and again, a wholistic approach, including the spiritual dimension as well as the others, leads to astonishing results in the care of terminally or incurably ill persons. Specialists in oncology work with psychotherapists and logotherapists in a reconciled and reconciling atmosphere. When patients who have been declared incurable are reconciled with themselves, their neighbors, with God, and reconciled also to their illnesses and the prospect of dying, the results are sometimes surprising. Life is given a new chance to prevail.

Chapter Two

CHRIST: THE GOOD SHEPHERD AND HEALER

Looking forward to the third millenium after Christ's coming, the Church needs, above all, to look to Christ, the Good Shepherd and Healer, and to commit herself to carrying out her mission to preach the Good News as an authentic image of Christ, the Good Shepherd and Divine Physician. The wounds to be healed are deep and terrifying. Will our healing faith and healing love be strong enough to embrace the healing power of our Savior, Jesus Christ?

Christ: The Good Shepherd

The image and role of Christ, Pastor and Healer, are beautifully predicted in the prophet Ezekiel. The Lord Yahweh says this:

"Now I myself will ask after my sheep and go in search of them. . . . I will feed them on good grazing-ground, and their pasture shall be the high mountains of Israel. I myself will tend my flock, I myself pen them in their fold, says the Lord GOD. I will search for the lost, recover the straggler, bandage the hurt, strengthen the sick, leave the healthy and strong to play, and give them their proper food" (Ezekiel 34:11-16).

This text is fulfilled in Jesus: "I am the good shepherd; the good shepherd lays down his life for the sheep. . . . I know my own sheep and my sheep know me" (John 10:11-14). In Jesus, Yahweh — the "I am" — is near to the sinner, the outcast, the sick, the downtrodden. He himself is our Helper and Healer. We can call upon him, entrust ourselves to him.

God is no stranger to our misery, our illnesses and sufferings. He comes to us as the "One-of-us" (Son of Man), foretold by the prophet and by prophetic events: " . . . he became their deliverer in all their troubles. It was no envoy, no angel, but he himself that delivered them . . . " (Isaiah 63:8-9).

Job, representing the outcast and untouchable, suffered most under the self-righteous judgment of the pious ones who came only to look down on him and to mark their distance from that "sinner." But what finally consoled him and put him on the road to healing was the faith experience of God's compassionate presence with him. Job comes to experience God as the Compassionate One who is touched by his suffering. God assures those who trust in him: "I will be with him in time of trouble" (Psalm 91:15).

Jesus, the Good Shepherd, takes upon himself the horrible suffering of those forsaken ones whom the judgmental religious men declare to be forsaken by God. Here we touch upon one of the most characteristic dimensions of Christ's healing ministry: he heals the lepers by touching them, giving them the healing experience of human love and divine presence. Similarly, he rescues men and women who were social outcasts, scorned by those who failed to see their own need of healing and redemption. Jesus treats the sinful women as persons, giving them back a sense of dignity. He does the same with the class of tax gatherers and others despised as "bad characters," "hopeless cases." He eats with the friends of the tax gatherer, Levi-Matthew, and even invites himself to the house of Zacchaeus, one of those who were looked upon as traitors and exploiters. In these instances Christ brings about a rebirth of healthy relationships. The person who accepts this healing gratefully does so with a new heart. This person is ready to convert, to make restitution, and to give loving service to the poor.

Jesus, who in his divinity and divine mission came from heaven, heals by his warm humanity. His unlimited compassion has nothing of that condescension which, in human history, has so often hurt and even further degraded the outcast. By his closeness and total solidarity with the unclean, the poor, the sinner, he reveals the true image of God, Father of all. Luke, the physician, translates for the Hellenistic world the word of Jesus found in Matthew: "Be compassionate as your Father is compassionate" (Luke 6:36). (The *New English Bible* comes close to this emphasis by translating Matthew 5:48 as: "There must be no limit to your goodness, as your heavenly Father's goodness knows no bounds.") This, in contrast to the Stoic's God who was thought to be "perfect" because he was unmoved by human misery — a God removed from sinful and passionate man!

The Japanese author, Kitamuri, has sound biblical reason for writing about "God's pains," God being deeply moved by our suffering and misery. J. Moltmann, a famous professor of systematic theology, entitled one of his books *The Crucified God*. This is an approach quite different from the kind of theology which emphasizes judgment and punitive justice. Pointing a finger at outcast sinners is extremely unlike Jesus our Savior and Healer who is the only authentic image of God.

The Church of the third millenium can be thought of and longed for only as a healing Church, a Church healing and judging not from above but as one who is, herself, a "wounded healer" trying to become ever more a sacrament, a true image of God's compassionate, healing love as revealed in Jesus Christ.

An indispensable criterion for the Church's presence in the world will be the saving solidarity of our Savior who thus shows us the Father:

> Yet on himself he bore our sufferings,
>   our torments he endured. . . .
> We had all strayed like sheep,
>   each of us had gone his own way;
> but the LORD laid upon him
>   the guilt of us all (Isaiah 53:4-6).

It is Jesus' mission, entrusted to him by the compassionate Father.

Christ: Our Savior and Healer

One of the most urgent tasks of the Church is to restore in her ministry and witness the blend between proclaiming the Good News and the healing of the sick which marked Christ's mission and witness. In Mark's Gospel, Jesus declares from the very outset that he has come to proclaim the Good News (Mark 1:38). Then follows the description of how he carried out this mission. While sharing the Good News, indeed sharing himself, Jesus casts out evil spirits, heals the sick, reintegrates the lepers into human society. There is no dichotomy between healing and preaching the gospel of salvation. While healing the sick he announces that the kingdom of God has come. The very way of sharing the Good News is by healing and the Gospel. Forgiving sins, healing from

27

the leprosy of sin and unforgiveness, he makes the crippled walk again (Mark 2:1-12 and Matthew 9:2).

To the disciples of John the Baptizer, Jesus explains that what they had seen and heard — the healings *and* the evangelization of the poor — are the sign that he is, indeed, the Messiah, the sign of the coming of God's kingdom (Luke 7:20-22; Matthew 11:2-6). Especially in Luke's Gospel the healing power of Jesus is not completely accepted and described until the ones who are healed and all the witnesses give glory to God, render thanks, and tell the Good News to everyone.

Many learned books and articles have been written about the miracles of Jesus, and some of their conclusions are relevant to the theme of this book. The biblical accounts of Jesus' healing activity differ greatly from the legends of pagan religions about their miracle workers. The stories of the latter are exotic, spectacular, while Jesus severely rejects the devil's attempt to seduce him to perform "showcase" miracles. He likewise rebukes the Pharisees and others who to test him "asked him to show them a sign from heaven" (Matthew 16:1).

Surely, the healing done by Jesus is also a proof of divine mission and power; but his healing miracles are, above all, signs of his divine-human love, a revelation of his compassionate love. Compassion is not only a motive but also a vehicle, a communication that energizes a person's own hidden resources. Even the vocabulary used by the evangelists is significant. The New Testament authors intentionally avoid expressions which emphasize the spectacular aspect, such as *taumasia* (stupendous events) or *teras* (extraordinary miracle). They prefer expressions like *ergon* (a work of deep meaning), *dynamis* (a mighty deed, energy), and *semeion* (a sign).

By healing, Jesus reveals himself as a friend of the sick and suffering. The way he meets people — putting his faith in them, awakening trust and hope, restoring in them a sense of dignity and value — has a wonderfully healing effect on the spiritual, psycho-somatic, and, indirectly, their somatic well-being. The sick and the sinners do not feel condemned or judged but loved, healed, and forgiven (see John 3:17, 12:47). There is a deeper sense in Jesus' declaration: "It is not the healthy that need a doctor, but the sick; I have not come to invite virtuous people, but to call sinners to repentance" (Luke 5:32). It is a call to turn to him with trust and to acquire a change of heart. Those who think they are not in need of conversion will fail to heed their Savior and Healer.

Christ, the living Gospel of salvation, did not do away with all suffering, did not dispense us from dying physically; but he deeply changed the meaning and experience of suffering and death. By accepting the grace and message of our Redeemer, we shall be spared many kinds of illness and suffering and freed from a senseless, frightening death. United with Christ we shall know that "in Christ Jesus the life-giving law of the Spirit has set you free from the law of sin and death" (Romans 8:2). In a saving communion with Christ and rooted in the community of salvation, we shall be able to live in healthy and healing relationships with God, with our neighbor, our community, and with ourselves. We shall heal what can be healed and give, or rather uncover, the meaning in what cannot be healed.

In many ways the Bible illustrates the profound relation be-tween salvation and health. One aspect is that healing is an essential part of the proclamation of the Good News. It is an effective sign foretelling the final victory over the reign of the Evil One, a victory that will be most visible in Jesus' death on a cross, "so that through death he might break the power of him who had death at his command, that is, the devil; and might liberate those who, through fear of death, had all their lifetime been in ser-vitude" (Hebrews 2:14-15).

For those who have alienated themselves and thus have become locked into the solidarity of sinfulness, the Evil One — who represents sin-solidarity itself — in many ways has at his command sickness, suffering, and death. But in view of full redemption through the death and Resurrection of Christ, the very fact of healing the sick and restoring to life — as in Lazarus' case — announces the final victory over sickness and death. Further, for those united with him, Christ takes away from suffering and death everything that involves the reign of evil. D. M. Stanley, S.J., in his *Salvation and Healing,* reminds us that whoever, in absolute truth, unites his suffering and death with Christ is freed from Satan's reign. The very suffering, together with healing, enters into the reign of salvation.

For the Church's ministry it is important to understand that Christ did not just tell people how to give new meaning to suffering and illness, comforting them only with the hope of heaven; rather, he did all this in the context of his healing love and power. Only by healing whatever can be healed, we — the Church — can help people to discover the meaning of suffering in saving solidarity with Christ and with the whole community of salvation. All our God-given charisms, all our faithfulness to the Gospel and to the ministry of healing partake of the truthful proclamation of salvation.

No one is excluded from Christ's redemption. Through the Incarnation, the redemption in Christ, and through the coming of the Holy Spirit, human nature has been marvelously restored. If, through faith and faithfulness to grace, we become healthy members of Christ's body, we become also a source of health for others. We discover in ourselves, and help others to discover in themselves, the spiritual resources which can be called the "inner doctor." Believing in the Redeemer of the whole human person, in all humanity throughout the entire world, we must unite our energies to promote healthy interhuman relationships, healthy life-styles through the healing of the civic community and care for ecological balance.

Christic: Our Living Gospel and Healing Love

Christ, opening his heart as the Living Gospel and Healing Love and thus reaching out for the suffering and the sinners, invites us to enter the kingdom of love and saving justice. He calls us to conversion, to a radical and total decision. He challenges us to change our hearts and urges us to make a clear choice. Those who have experienced the nearness of the Emmanuel and the power of his healing love, and thereby have begun to understand his Gospel and himself as the living Gospel, feel attracted by the prospect of healing. But the decision to receive Christ should be based not so much on him as healer and liberator from suffering, but as bearer of salvation and thus also of healing. The sick should open themselves to their Savior and Healer in grateful faith; they should not lock themselves up in their own misery, ungratefully refusing faith and neglecting salvation while longing only for health in the narrowest sense.

Jesus does not ask for faith by command or beg it by bestowing benefits on the sick. He is himself the prototype of unlimited faith by which he accepts his mission from the Father, and in its fulfillment he suffers with the sufferers and bears the burden of the burdened. In his twofold mission to reveal to mankind the saving justice and healing compassion of the Father, he is wounded by the refusal of faith and love. He does not seek suffering; yet, in the cry of the blind, the sick, and the sinner, he hears the voice of the Father, even when he is nailed to the Cross. And Jesus, who has healed so many, remains on his Cross to call them to salvation.

This call to salvation coming from Christ, the living Gospel and loving Healer, is essentially a call to *faith,* understood in its full meaning as total commitment and surrender to Christ. The way to faith is marked by crises, just as the way to being healed and becoming whole leads through creative crises. Otherwise, the healing powers will be "aborted."

31

Faced with Christ who is himself the Glad News and Healing Love, each person must decide whether he or she will respond with an authentic "Yes," a truthful, faithful "Amen": that is, with living faith. If those who wish to experience healing love do so selfishly, seeking only earthly well-being, they practically guarantee that they will not receive healing and saving love. By separating health from salvation they fail not only in their search for salvation but also in their pursuit of healing and wholeness. They also deprive those around them of the witness of faith and gratitude. Therefore, Jesus cannot tell them "Your faith has saved you," as he told the leper who returned to him to thank him and to praise God by spreading the good news everywhere.

Not only those who directly experience the healing love and power of Jesus but also all those who witness this event of God's powerful presence (or even those who hear of it) are called to a decision of faith: to salvation. They, too, have to go through a crisis. Just as in Christ the offer of salvation and healing cannot be separated, so the faith response should not be to either health alone or to transcendental salvation alone. Christ calls for a total response in openness to salvation *and* health, for loving adoration of God, for healthy personal relationships, and for entrance into the kingdom of God — which is also a kingdom of saving justice and healing love.

Both the sick person, to whom Christ has offered salvation, forgiveness, and, at the same time, healing, and those who have witnessed the nearness of the Emmanuel take a great risk when they refuse a total response. By aborting the creative crisis they fall further away from salvation and the joy of faith, more than ever affected by unhealthy relationships, more constricted by the unsavory powers in the world around them.

It is true that Christ did not come to judge but to save and to heal, but it is also true that the way people respond to his coming and his healing presence reveals their secret thoughts (see Luke 2:35).

Some are thereby saved by faith; others pass judgment on themselves by their own refusal of faith.

The same is true for the Church's mission. Wherever those sent by Christ to proclaim the Good News and to heal the sick radiate both the joy of the Gospel and healing love and service, people are effectively called to faith, to salvation in all its dimensions, including a higher level of wholeness, healthier personal and social relationships, a more wholesome life-style, and a healthier community life.

By its inner dynamics, the crisis through which people go is meant to be creative; yet it can be abortive if they desire to separate salvation from healthy human interrelationships, if they cling to their hope of heaven but not their personal share of responsibility for justice and peace on earth or, conversely, if they want earthly well-being but not conversion to the God of love and peace.

Christ: Our Redeemer

For a distinctive Catholic spirituality, faith in redemption calls for us to thank God not only for redemption itself but also for the mystery of creation. God loves everything that he has created. Even after the Fall, the human person remained marked by the fact that God created us to his own image and likeness. The mystery of the Incarnation, death, and Resurrection of Christ proclaims forever that God loves what he has created, and what has fallen and been wounded is even more wonderfully re-created.

Only sin, stubborn resistance to the Redeemer and to the grace of the Holy Spirit, can prevent a person from accepting redemption. The redeemed discover wonderful resources within themselves. Christ shows all how these resources can be awakened and strengthened. As Redeemer and Healer, he calls for cooperation and, above all, for faith, which is the joyous and grateful acceptance of his saving and healing love. If we allow Christ to set us free for himself and his heavenly Father, we can, in creative liberty, become co-workers in his mission of redemption. We can become healthy and healing members of his Body. We can become light for the world.

Paul, the apostle, experienced the healing and renewing power of the Redeemer who rescued him from self-righteousness; he senses how the whole creation eagerly expects a share in the liberty of the children of God (see Romans 8:19-23). We still suffer from temptations that arise from within and are reinforced by the world around us. We are in danger of being wounded by other peoples' frustrations; we suffer and are sickened because of unhealthy relationships and unjust structures. But meeting Christ, the Redeemer, in grateful and trustful faith, we come to grasp our mission to share the good news of redemption by healing people, by helping them to discover their hidden resources and to open themselves to the work of the Spirit, who renews our hearts and the face of the world.

We see how the world around us is partially enslaved by ideologies and idols, by consumerism, by greed, sex exploitation, and many other forms of destructive behavior which spread unhealthiness in many ways. If we believe the gospel of redemption, we can join our forces and our witness of love, as individuals and as faith-filled communities, to contribute greatly to healing wounds: wounded hearts, wounded memories, wounded relationships. We can give witness by wholesome convictions and a healthy lifestyle. We can promote worldwide justice, healing, and peace.

If we Christians would join hands and talents, we surely could free humanity in a very short time from the plague of leprosy which still distresses more than 25 million people. And while doing this, by small but specific sacrifices — refraining from cigarette smoking and other damaging habits — we could start healing more and more facets of our sickly society and culture.

34

The first condition for all this is knowing Christ, the Redeemer and Healer, rendering thanks for the gift of redemption, building up faith communities, and accepting our mission as healers of the sick, friends and helpers of the needy, the lonely, and the aged.

In our Creed we honor Christ as Redeemer of the world. We honor him in truth when together we take care that public opinion, legislation, politics, and the ecology of this world remain healthy. As Christians, we learn from the Gospel that healing has to rise from our hearts because we have turned totally to Christ and his reign of love.

Christ: Our Reconciler

Christ, our Redeemer and Reconciler, came into a world filled with hatred, ill will, unforgiveness, anger, and war. Because human relationships were miserable, people made each other ever more miserable. Into this world Christ brought the message that his Father is compassionate and merciful, willing to reconcile all to himself and among themselves. And Christ gave the supreme manifestation and proof of this reconciling love on the Cross: "Father, forgive!"

Christ's own compassionate and healing love together with his good news that conversion, forgiveness, and peace are possible make us sinners deeply aware that we are in need of divine forgiveness. From this awareness comes a new spirit, a new heart, with the utmost readiness to forgive others just as the heavenly Father forgives and heals the wounds of our own sins.

Christ, the Healer, made two important points clear. First, none of us may look down on a sick or suffering person and consider him or her a greater sinner than we "others" are. We should learn from the Divine Physician to heal and not to judge. Second, Christ, by combining healing with proclaiming the good news that conversion is possible and urgent, impressively teaches us that unforgiven sins and unwillingness to forgive each other are the chief sources of misery, of unhealthy personal relationships, and of many kinds of sickness. He has thoroughly demonstrated the intimate connection between actual healing and forgiving sins and leading people to forgive wholeheartedly.

The Gospel of Mark, which from the very first chapter gives prominence to the healing ministry of Christ, underlines this fusion of forgiving sins and healing. Christ surprises everyone when he tells the paralytic man who is brought to him for healing: "My son, your sins are forgiven" (Mark 2:5). With word and sign Jesus explains the mysterious connection: "Is it easier to say to this paralysed man, 'Your sins are forgiven', or to say, 'Stand up, take your bed, and walk'? But to convince you that the Son of Man has the right on earth to forgive sins" — he turned to the paralysed man — "I say to you, 'stand up, take your bed, and go home' " (Mark 2:9-11).

This text and the whole manner in which Jesus combined healing and the proclamation of the good news of conversion and reconciliation raise complex theological and pastoral questions about the mission and power of the Church to forgive sins.

Here are some of the main questions to be asked. Should not the sacrament of Reconciliation be seen and practiced in the broader context of healing forgiveness? Is the experience of healing forgiveness in the life of the faithful and of the whole Church perhaps a condition for the credibility of the Church's power to forgive sins? Would not the whole pastoral ministry, and particularly the celebration of the sacrament of Reconciliation, be more meaningful if their therapeutic dimensions were more emphasized? Should there not be a more impelling connection between proclamation by word and sacrament and the whole practice of forgiveness and reconciliation for all sinners who come with good will? Should we not fear more the scandal of excluding people of good will from the full experience of forgiveness than the foreseeable reaction of people who are inclined to be scandalized when sinners, whose sins are different from theirs, are reconciled not on the basis of fulfillment of the law but on the basis of divine graciousness and good will? Should we not all have a livelier realization and bring others to the same realization that the unwillingness to practice healing forgiveness is the greatest obstacle to reconciliation, health, and peace?

Immediately after the prophetic story of healing forgiveness and healing-by-forgiveness, Mark's Gospel gives a report which characterizes in a unique way the prophetic and healing ministry of Christ. When Jesus invites the tax gatherer, Levi-Matthew, into his intimate fellowship, Levi-Matthew, thus honored, comes to a surprising and illuminating conclusion. He prepares a meal for Jesus, to which he invites his old friends, other tax gatherers and "bad characters." Following the "logic of the heart" he thinks, "I am no better than these others, and since Jesus calls me, he will surely accept them equally."

This prophetic messianic meal with Levi and his cronies, who are now becoming Jesus' friends, is a scandal for all the self-righteous, who do not realize how sick they themselves are and how remote they are from the liberating and healing truth. Jesus tells them that he "did not come to invite virtuous people, but sinners"; but unless the self-righteous adherents to a sterile orthodoxy realize that they, too, are both sinners and sick people, they will never participate in the messianic meal and never understand the biblical virtues of humility, gentleness, nonviolence, graciousness, and healing compassion.

Ministers of the sacrament of Reconciliation, as well as other believers, can be healers with Christ only to the extent that they follow the example of Levi-Matthew, understanding themselves as "wounded healers" in need of healing forgiveness and being gradually healed from the temptation to act as self-righteous judges. A humility like that of the newly converted Levi-Matthew allows us to enter the realm of liberating and healing truth: that is, to know and to make known Christ, the Reconciler and Healer.

After having stretched out his arms, opened his heart, and prayed for us all — "Father forgive them" — Jesus sends his apostles to bring, through the power of the Holy Spirit, the messianic peace and forgiveness of sins to all people (John 20:19-22). Those who, with abiding gratitude, accept forgiveness and peace from Christ become his authorized messengers and ministers of healing forgiveness — each of course in accord with individual charisms given. But for all, there is the absolute condition that, with heart and mind and will and with all their attitudes and behavior, they pray, "Forgive us the wrong we have done, as we have forgiven those who have wronged us" (Matthew 6:12).

We cannot grow in the joy of salvation, in spiritual and psychic health, and become effective signs of Christ the Healer unless we are constantly and gratefully aware that we live by God's saving justice and healing compassion, and unless we make this awareness an unconditional law for our own attitude toward others and toward our ministry of reconciliation. Without this conscious gratitude and fundamental option, we are unable to know Christ and to follow him. We therefore cannot fulfill the mission to proclaim the Good News and to heal the sick, a mission entrusted to all true believers. And we are even useless in the quest for true orthodoxy, for "the unloving know nothing of God" (1 John 4:8).

The more we show our gratitude for the undeserved gift of forgiveness and peace, the closer we can come to the biblical virtues of vigilance, discernment, hope, and gentleness. We become reconcilers and peacemakers, heralds of the Good News and thus can say, "Peace on earth to all men of good will."

There is a considerable amount of literature today on the many people who become sick and are a source of frustration for others because they are nourishing grudges and bitterness in their hearts.

They are unable to cultivate healthy and healing relationships with others and, more than any other group, are vulnerable to illnesses of a psychosomatic nature, such as stress and heart attack. On the other hand, full reconciliation with God, with neighbor, and with oneself, a gentleness and readiness for healing forgiveness greatly increase the chances to overcome not only psychosomatic but even somatic illnesses.

A "Eucharistic memory," filled with praise for the wondrous deeds of God and thankfulness for all his gifts and all our experiences with gracious people, is an inexhaustible source of health and healing and, perhaps, the best contribution for the work of peace on all levels. Christ, the Good Shepherd, the Healer, our Peace, has taught us this clearly and emphatically. We can only wonder why we are such poor learners in this field while learning so easily many less important facts.

The arms race, the nuclear threat, M.A.D. (mutually assured destruction), the age-old tendency to undermine the opposition are spreading distrust, hatred, enmity — all a result of self-righteousness and lust for power. Whole nations are sick, anguished, bitter. Without a change of heart on all levels, diplomatic negotiations will not resolve these awe-full problems. Their deadly wounds can be healed only by going to the roots of the evil and learning from Christ how to become peacemakers and healers.

The disciples of Christ should be the first to use the remedies offered us by our Redeemer: the biblical healing virtues. The great Mahatma Gandhi described them in the biblical sense as *satyagraha:* healing truth, the force of truth whose heart is love. Those who live by this truth make the opposition their partners in dialogue and in the search for the next possible step toward fuller justice, peace, and truth-force. The *Satyagrahi* do not look on enemies as people to be destroyed or dishonored. They help their opponents to discover their own inner resources: indeed, to discover themselves as brothers of all, seeking their own and other peoples' well-being by justice, sharing, and by healing for-giveness, without any attitude of condescension.

The *Satyagrahi* realize how much undeserved esteem they have received and receive constantly from God. Thus they are able to credit their opponents with the same esteem, letting them know that they trust that they have just as much goodness to be dis-covered and to become effective in a common search for justice, truth, and peace. Nonviolent resistance confronts, first of all, the basic evils: self-righteousness, hatred, contempt for others, the spreading of subversive propaganda, lust for power and for victory over others even to the demonic point of demanding "uncon-ditional surrender."

Today the *satyagraha* alternative, as a new spirit with new strategies, has become a focal point of genuine evangelization, healing ministry, and peace mission. The time is over when separation between the teaching of dogmatic truth on one hand and healing ministry on the other can be considered tolerable. Apart from the biblical virtues of nonviolence and peacefulness there can exist no faithful and effective evangelization and pastoral work. Of late, I have met people who, through the witness of Pax Christi groups and the "gospel of peace and reconciliation," have become interested in Christ and have come to know and to love him.

The Church's growth in the next millenium will be measured by her ministry of healing justice, compassionate love, nonviolence, and by the extent to which she lives her mission to proclaim the gospel of peace credibly in a complete union of pastoral care and healing love. She can help humankind not only to survive but to survive with dignity and under healthier conditions when she lives and proclaims that joyous faith, that total faith commitment and love, those biblical virtues which typify healing power. She can be what she is meant to be and to become, ever more and on all levels, a sacrament, an effective and convincing sign of reconciliation and healing faith.

Christ's Spirit: Giver of Life

In today's world we often hear the terms "health delivery" and "health industry." But neither salvation nor truly human health can be bought and delivered; they are not products of either industry or ecclesiastical "administration," and surely not of unspirited "administration" of sacraments.

Christ calls us to salvation and truly human health, inviting us to himself, offering us the experience of his presence, his graciousness, his saving truth and healing love. The kind of healing that points to salvation has to arise from within. Christ, who calls us to intimate friendship — which is the most healing relationship — sends us his Spirit to awaken and enliven our "inner doctor," our own inner resources.

Trusting in Christ and in the life-giving Spirit, we can face the shadowy forces around us and the shades within us. Our Creator and Redeemer shares with us intense energies, a deep longing for salvation, for integrity, and for truly human health of body, mind, and spirit. It behooves the Church to help us to discover these resources and to show us how to make good use of them.

Carl Gustav Jung proposes this rule for therapists: "The best we can do is to give the inner doctor, who dwells in each patient, a chance to become operative." In a much higher way, this is the rule for the Church's pastoral care and healing ministry: to help the faithful to rely on God's grace and, in that trust, to discover their own inner resources. That means to believe in the Holy Spirit, the giver of life, and to live according to the law of the Spirit who gives us life in Christ Jesus (see Romans 8:2).

Just as we can stop relying on "health industry" and "health delivery" and assume responsibility for our own health through a wholesome life-style and a good human milieu, even more so should we give up seeking false securities and entrust ourselves to the Spirit. His law is written in our hearts and can be grasped by grateful people whose lives are marked by adoration of the Father, the Son and the Holy Spirit: adoration proven truthful by healing love.

Christ, our Good Shepherd and Healer, has promised us the Paraclete. The Church, professing her faith in the saving and healing power of the Holy Spirit, is a joyous Church, a singing Church. With the apostle of the Gentiles, she dares to tell us by all her life and ministry: "You are no longer under law, but under the grace of God" (Romans 6:14).

This surely does not mean abolishment of the decalogue. What it does mean is that the Church shows us, by word and example, the way of the Beatitudes and directs us to the supreme criteria chosen by those who let themselves be guided by the life-giving Spirit: " . . . the harvest of the Spirit is love, joy, peace, patience, kindness, goodness, fidelity, gentleness, and self-control. . . . If the Spirit is the source of our life, let the Spirit also direct our course" (Galatians 5:22-25). Those who trustfully live on this level and, with God's help, try to live ever more faithfully on this level are hope-inspiring signs of salvation, peace, and health.

The world of today is in dire need of these healing believers who fulfill the mission entrusted to them by Christ and his prophecy: "Faith will bring with it these miracles: believers will cast out devils in my name . . . and the sick on whom they lay their hands will recover" (Mark 16:17-18).

There are many evil spirits in our culture, in our economic framework, in our politics, and in our civic community. Many wounds cry out for healing. The world needs holy healers who recognize themselves humbly as "wounded healers" and put their trust in God.

Chapter Three

OUR REVEALING-HEALING MISSION

When we try to understand the full mission of the Church, her true nature and purpose, we must always keep in mind that it is infinitely more than a mandated external institution. Above all, it is a wondrous sharing in the very mystery of Christ and his mission from the Father.

The fulfillment of the sublime mission, to proclaim the Good News and to heal, requires a complete incorporation into Christ, the Revealer and Healer. The Church cannot know herself and her mission without lovingly knowing Christ, and she cannot know Christ without being attentive to his ways.

Christ accomplishes his mission to reveal and to heal in a thoroughly unexpected way. He brings to it a new kind of authority, the prophetic authority of the Servant, which should characterize the Church also. And he is Savior and Healer at the same time because of his total readiness to fulfill his mission in extreme suffering and humiliation.

(In this section I am particularly indebted to P. S. Minear's *To Heal and to Reveal: The Prophetic Vocation According to Luke*.)

Sharing in the authority of the Servant-Messiah

One of the strongest reasons for the power and authority of Jesus, as Revealer, Savior, and Healer, is his humble obedience to the Father and to the Holy Spirit, who came visibly upon him when he was baptized in the Jordan. Consecrated and sent by the Holy Spirit, he established an unending solidarity of salvation with sick and sinful humankind. By the same Spirit, Christ is driven into the desert and strengthened to fight victoriously against Satan's most dangerous temptations. By his firm "no" to the temptation to seek and to offer material security, his "no" to show-off religion and vanity, and his final "no" to any kind of power or authority linked with the "prince of this dark world" of power and violence, Jesus shows us how to remove the main obstacles from our participation in his revealing-healing mission. He paves the way for us to salvation and healing.

Empowered by the Holy Spirit, Jesus purposefully chooses to live a life of austere poverty and to guide himself by a new kind of authority, manifesting the coming of God's reign. It is the authority of the "Servant of God," Servant of the poor, of the outcast, the sick and downtrodden, indeed, the Servant of all. By this irrevocable decision Jesus drives out the evil spirits. He drives away Satan.

Under the influence of "the authorities and potentates of this dark world" (Ephesians 6:12), who poison the atmosphere of human existence, humankind is greatly disturbed in all its basic relationships by domineering styles of authority: arrogance, exploitation, oppression, manipulation, and deception. If such authority is exercised in the name of religion, the damage to human relationships and human health, as well as to structures and authority itself, is even more severe.

The coming of the kingdom of God in the messianic era is specifically marked by a new healing kind of authority embodied in Jesus. Jesus knows that he is sent by the Father and consecrated by the Spirit to reveal and exercise the authority of the healing Servant. The Gospel is most explicit on this point. After the visible descent of the Spirit on Jesus during his baptism a heavenly voice is heard to say: "Thou art my Son, my Beloved" (Luke 3:22), clearly bringing to mind the great prophecy about the Servant of God (Isaiah 42:1). Later, Jesus calls our attention to the same truth (Luke 4:18). Then, immediately, he begins to proclaim the Good News and to heal.

But what matters directly here is that Jesus teaches his apostles and disciples most emphatically that their mission to share in the proclamation of the Good News and the healing of the sick presupposes the same fundamental option for simplicity and humble service (Luke 9:3, 10:3ff). Their whole conduct should show that they are not ashamed of the firm purpose of the Son of Man to be and to act as the Servant.

When the seventy-two came back from their first preaching-and-healing journey and exultantly reported that even devils submitted to them, Jesus told them to rejoice, rather, "that your names are enrolled in heaven" (Luke 10:17-20). This calls for a totally new way of life according to the heavenly design as it became visible in Jesus himself. It becomes even more evident when he praises the Father for having revealed his mysteries only to the humble ones who are conformed with him and to whom the Father reveals himself completely (Luke 10:21-24). Invested with the same servant authority, the disciples can "see," and thus reveal and heal.

This instruction of the disciples and their introduction into the mystery of salvation and the new kind of authority take place on Jesus' journey toward Jerusalem, where his final and supreme revelation of the authority of the Servant will be made on the Cross.

Jesus' self-revelation as the Servant and his instruction of the disciples happen in the context of a healing from blindness. The disciples, too, are still blind, until they recognize the healing-revealing power of the Servant authority and willingly become servants with him. Thus assimilated to Jesus' humility, simplicity, and poverty and invested with the same authority, they become prophets, healers, heralds of the Good News.

Jesus fulfills his healing-revealing mission in the service of the poor, the beggars, and especially of those who recognize themselves as poor sinners in need of God's mercy. He makes himself one of the poor, one of those who have no power — having rejected the old authority structures. He is One-of-us in all things except sin.

The messengers of salvation and the prophets of the new covenant are, therefore, essentially called to become like beggars, like the humblest of servants. They are not to worry about material security or provisions, and are to be fully aware that they are in need of redemption and healing. Only thus do they know they are invited to the messianic meal, and only thus do they become wholly open to the healing power and authority of Jesus.

In Luke's Gospel the truth that the poor receive salvation and liberation through the saving authority of the Servant-Messiah is in the forefront, while the healing of the sick becomes the privileged sign of that basic change in the meaning and style of authority. Once we have understood that "salvation is destined only for beggars and sinners," we can safely conclude that Christ likes to impart salvation and healing through prophets and servants who are even humbler than those beggars, sinners, and sufferers.

In this light, the biblical narrative about the disciples' striking inability to heal the epileptic (Luke 9:37-40) becomes very revealing. They do not seem to understand. All of them, including Peter, refuse to accept that Christ's mission must be carried out by him as a most humble Servant. In consequence, they do not see the need for self-denial and conformation with the Servant-Messiah. Therefore, Jesus in anguish exclaims: "What an unbelieving and perverse generation! How long shall I be with you and endure you all?" (Luke 9:41) The same kind of perversity reappears in reprehensible form during the Last Supper when "a jealous dispute broke out: who among them should rank highest?" Jesus teaches them by word and example: "Here am I among you like a servant" (Luke 22:24,27).

When we ask ourselves about the causes of the long-lasting crisis in the ministry of salvation and the healing service of the Church in the light of Luke's Gospel, we cannot evade the issue by talking about new strategies and tactics. Our first effort must be to conform ourselves with the Servant-Messiah and the authority manifested by his humility. We must earnestly renounce and oppose that false authority understanding which Satan dared to suggest to Jesus (see Matthew 4:10). And we cannot ignore one of the most startling scenes of the Gospel which pictures Jesus using almost identical words of wrath as he rebukes Peter, who has protested against his Master's being the Servant-Messiah: "Away with you, Satan" (see Matthew 16:23).

Sharing in the power of Christ

As he heals the sick and proclaims the Good News, Jesus, in a deep mystical sense, treads the road to Jerusalem, on the way to the

Cross, knowing that the shocking history of the murder of past prophets will be reenacted in him (see Matthew 23:33-39). His suffering, death, and Resurrection become the inexhaustible fountain of redemption and healing love for all generations.

The compassion with which Jesus evangelized the poor and healed the sick does not reveal its true meaning until we view it as part of his readiness to accept the bitter suffering of his own Passion.

"Blessed" is the name Jesus calls those of his disciples who practice childlike humility because, freed from all spiritual blindness, they will "see" what the Father reveals in him (Luke 10:21-24). But he also expects them to be able to radiate the joy of redemption when they share in his suffering and persecution (Matthew 5:10-12). Thus they become healing witnesses molded by his "blessed suffering" and his Resurrection.

By the active compassion revealed in his salvation and healing of the suffering, the sick, and sinners, Jesus shows us the true countenance of the Father. This revelation reaches its peak when on the Cross he prays, "Abba, Father, forgive them!" and then entrusts his spirit to his loving Father. He suffered so much because his compassion was so great.

In the words of P. S. Minear, "modern disciples need the kind of training in suffering which Jesus provided for his followers. It was by way of sharing in the messianic sufferings that followers would recognize the powerful presence of the new age in the redemptive activity of Jesus." By imitating the compassion and sufferings of Jesus, the sufferings of his disciples — especially those endured in their ministry — also become a source of healing power. Minear concludes: "It was the therapeutic power of messianic suffering which distinguished exorcisms and cures in the New Testament from ancient hellenistic wonder stories as well as from modern faith-healing by revivalist preachers."

Only by entering fully into the mystery of salvation, by which the endurance of human weakness in union with Jesus' messianic suffering becomes a channel of God's power, can we conceive of the healing power bestowed by God on faithful disciples who follow Christ the Servant, the suffering Messiah.

The radiating joy and peace of messengers of salvation even in the midst of suffering and persecution, the constant praise by those who have been healed and by all redeemed people who experience wholesome and healing relationships — all this points to the mystery of the Passion and Resurrection of Christ. This is the overall theme of the Acts of the Apostles and the Letters of Saint Paul. Time and again it is reanimated in the lives of the saints who were and are totally dedicated to the ministry of salvation and have received the charism of healing in the broadest sense.

This biblical vision and the wisdom acquired from the lives of the saints present a great challenge to the whole Church. The People of God must know that they cannot fulfill the unified mission to be witnesses of the Good News and healers of humanity without entering wholeheartedly into the luminous cloud of messianic humility and suffering. We must constantly remind ourselves that we are faced not with an imperative imposed from without, but with the innermost sharing in the mystery of Christ who is the living Gospel and the divine-human Physician.

Chapter Four

HEALING MISSION OF TODAY'S CHURCH

Before writing this chapter, I read — among others — two recently published books that I hoped would provide some insights on my theme. *Christ Proclaimed,* by Franz Jozef van Beeck, S.J., and *The Church: All-embracing Sacrament of Salvation,* by Johann Auer, were highly praised. Although their titles offered great promise, neither one was of much help. The first book fails to emphasize the healing activity of Christ as part of his revealing love, and the second fails to face the Church's mission to heal as part of the mystery of salvation.

I am afraid that this situation is indicative of a widespread omission, revealing grave shortcomings both in soteriology and Christology. Christ, the Savior, cannot be faithfully proclaimed and the Church cannot be really understood and made visible if her mission to heal — in combination with her mission to save — is ignored.

What must be stressed is the enduring unity of healing and revealing. If these dimensions are separated or divorced, both "partners" suffer equally: the ministry for salvation and the ministry of healing.

Since we seek creative fidelity for the present moment, the Church must first ask: What are the most pressing needs of today's world, of men and women of our time, in view of salvation and healing? This will then be followed by the fundamental question: How can the Church, in faithfulness to her identity and integral mission, respond to these needs in full awareness of the intimate relationship of salvation, wholeness, and truly human health?

Making salvation fully visible

The Church has the mission *to be* and to become ever more visibly and effectively a sacrament, *"a visible, efficacious sign"* of salvation in its entirety, in all its dimensions. The sacramentality of the Church is not just an abstract ideal: her entire essence, her complete dynamics, her very countenance, her total witness, prayer life, and celebrations, together with her preaching and teaching combine to make her truly real. And this means that she also must gear herself to the full concept and reality of salvation.

In an era of Cartesian dualism, we spoke glibly of "pastors of souls," overstressing "souls" and their salvation in heaven. Today, there is a strong and sometimes equally one-sided reaction against this verticalism and dualism. Some seem to see only the horizontal dimension of human well-being and justice.

Against this new trend, salvation must be emphasized as coming from God and leading to God and his everlasting kingdom. This is the primary goal to be sought; then all the rest will follow. Of course, this does not at all minimize our commitment to justice and peace or to the wholeness of the human being, healthy relationships, integrity, and health. These goals cannot be reached unless we root ourselves in the whole of the reality and message of the kingdom of God. Once we set our priorities we cannot indulge in dichotomy.

The vitality of the Church's human-social image and even of her fulfillment of the supreme ministry of salvation depend to a certain degree on the health of the society and culture within which the People of God live: the healthiness of their life-style, community convictions, civic and family life. Therefore, it is an integral part of the Church's salvific mission that she should care for healthy and healing human relationships on all levels. People's health, their capacity to open themselves to all dimensions of the messianic peace and to commit themselves to spreading the gospel of peace and salvation, has much to do with the Church's ministry of salvation and its integration of revealing and healing.

The dichotomy between verticalism and horizontalism, which today tends to split the Church, cannot be checked unless pastors and all the faithful recognize that salvation, in its fullness, includes care for the *wholeness and health of individuals* and of the *civic community.* We all have to understand that we cannot proclaim the grace of salvation without becoming healthier from within and helping each other to find the full meaning of life, health, and salvation.

Forming a reconciling-healing community

The Church is a community of salvation and a healing-saving sacrament of reconciliation, coming from the Lord as an undeserved gift and continuing as a mission and task for the People of God. To attain inner health and unity she must appeal to many different kinds of people. The more she appreciates and liberates the variety of charisms and the many different cultures and traditions, the more she becomes the health-giving and saving sacrament she is meant to be.

The healing mission entrusted by Christ to the Church is not something she can simply turn over to a chosen professional group or institution. She herself must be and become ever more a healing force as a community of salvation and of healthy, saving relationships.

Here we might mention just one historical example which can be discussed frankly today, since conditions are improving. If a Latin Western Church, claiming universal jurisdiction, makes or proposes to make Latin language and Latin culture the rule of conduct and criterion for all under her jurisdiction, she not only hurts and alienates other cultures but makes Latin culture itself less healthy, more arrogant, and poorer. The Church herself becomes sick, tending to imprison the mystery of God and salvation within categories that are culturally too narrow, thereby greatly diminishing her Gospel-proclaiming capacity and the necessary discernment between the substance of revelation and time-and-place-bound terminologies, symbols, and structures. As a result, the Church would seriously weaken and even betray her mission to reconcile cultures and nations and to lead them to an enriching and reconciling dialogue. Thus, too, she would greatly jeopardize her total peace mission.

Consistent faithfulness to the doctrine that before God there is no difference between Jew, Greek, and barbarian is part and parcel of the "sound doctrine" of which the pastoral letters speak so insistently (1 Timothy 1:3f, 4:3, 4:6, 6:3; 2 Timothy 4:3; Titus 1:13, 1:9, 2:2). For the author of the pastoral letters, nothing is more damaging for the faith community than intolerant quarrels about man-made traditions, taboos, and prohibitions. "Go on reminding people of this, and charge them solemnly before God to stop disputing about mere words; it does no good, and is the ruin of those who listen" (2 Timothy 2:14). Anyone who does not "give his mind to wholesome precepts . . . I call him a pompous ignoramus. He is morbidly keen on mere verbal questions and quibbles" (1 Timothy 6:3-4).

In order to be a healing force, a faith community should be deeply rooted in knowledge of Jesus, in wholesome doctrine, and invigorated by healthy and healing intercommunal relationships and practices, including keen appreciation of special charisms of healing. But the basic healing activity is continuous as is diligent reconciliation within the parish community and through it the community at large. A reconciled and reconciling community will be ever attentive to a solidaric commitment for healing the sick and for their loving care.

Good Catholic teaching has always emphasized the uniqueness of each person. To weaken or hamper this uniqueness infects both those who impose it and those who are exposed to such deviations. But it is equally true that individual persons cannot reach their own full identity and integration without realizing and affirming their rootedness in the community by active co-responsibility. Those who establish a balance between uniqueness and solidarity are healing and reconciling agents.

The sick person is part of his or her family relationship and environment. Any chance for physical, psychic, and spiritual health depends to a great extent on the spirit of responsibility and cooperation on all sides, including the sick person who should never consider himself or herself as a mere recipient, dependent on others.

A community that has a deep understanding of the salvific value of redeemed suffering — a redeemed way of dealing with sickness — will not only help the sick more effectively but will also benefit from the example and prayer of those who have accepted the challenge of sickness.

We cannot cope with suffering in its naked reality. Of itself, it is not a source of joy or strength. But suffering, interpreted as redemptive expression of love and transfigured by the love of Christ, becomes the strongest expression of human solidarity, within the mysterious solidarity of God — through Christ — with us. When the apostle to the Gentiles made this discovery, he exulted: "It is now my happiness to suffer for you. . . . To complete, in my poor human flesh, the full tale of Christ's afflictions still to be endured, for the sake of his body which is the church" (Colossians 1:24).

During my life I have had several opportunities to see how believers make this same discovery and how deeply it changes their lives and even their suffering. Here is one example:

Sometimes I celebrate the Eucharist in the room of our Brother Alphonse, who has been bedridden for more than twenty years and is now unable even to feed himself. One day when he was in great pain, I suggested at the beginning of the Mass: "Imagine, now, Christ coming in person and asking you to make a choice: either you regain your health so you will be able to work for the community with all your well-known skill (in which case you would still gain heaven, but alone), or you continue to suffer, uniting all your pain with Christ's suffering, and then at the hour of your death Christ comes in his glory and shows you a great crowd of people who, through your faith, your suffering, your patience and cheerfulness, you have inspired and helped to reach salvation. Which of these would you choose?" Alphonse's response was immediate: "The latter!" I knew that our Brother had made this choice a long time ago, but reaffirming it changed his whole countenance and appeased to some extent his pain, which he then brought into the Eucharistic celebration.

The inspiration so often given by the sick is a precious gift to all.

And the constant care for the sick, the regular and loving visits with them, the meaningful celebration of the Anointing of the Sick — all these promote the salvation, integrity, and wholeness of the community itself.

Dr. R. A. Lambourne (in his book *Community, Church and Healing*) has given marked attention to this insight and has deepened its theological perspective. He views illness and healing within the sphere of the Passion and Resurrection of Christ. "A sick person is joined to the Body of Christ. He is joined to the fellowship of Christ, the fellowship of the Holy Spirit and the fellowship of the saints. He is joined to the fellowship of love — the fellowship of love which is to be found in the local church, and which, embracing the suffering of its own members and the suffering in its neighborhood, is to be a therapeutic community."

The Church is meant to be a reliable image of Christ, whose whole redeeming presence and activity is therapeutic, liberating, healing. He shows us that those who seek themselves and their lives selfishly, staying as far away as possible from the suffering of others, lose their true self, waste their lives. "Here, indeed," Dr. Lambourne concludes, "is a mystery proclaimed in the life of Christ. He who would be made whole must suffer as he joins the suffering of man in Christ."

In his beautiful apostolic letter *Salvifici Doloris,* John Paul II gives equal importance to the two directions in which true believers approach the various forms of suffering. There are those who become followers of the merciful Samaritan, Christ himself, by healing and caring, fighting injustice, and healing individual and collective wounds. And there are those who are suffering and, in their own outstanding way, become merciful Samaritans by sharing in Christ's suffering, imitating the kind of solidaric love that Christ had when he accepted his suffering.

The pope emphasizes that the suffering of the disciples of Christ is not only redeemed but enters creatively into the history and dynamics of redemption. "By bringing redemption through suffering, Christ has elevated human suffering unto the level of redemption. . . . Therefore, in his suffering man can become sharer of Christ's redeeming suffering" (#19). The believer does this by entering fully into the healing and saving love of Christ while accepting this great challenge and test in the fellowship of disciples. Hence, the pope appeals to these sufferers: "We ask you who are weak to become a source of strength for the Church" (# 31).

Christian community education — a deep understanding of the community of salvation through liturgy, teaching, preaching experienced by the entire Church community — provides a good foundation for healthy relationships everywhere. It raises the consciousness level of each person, reminding all of their responsibility for their own health (always in view of the health of the whole Body of Christ) and for active co-responsibility in preventing illness and promoting the health of all, including the healing of the civic community.

From a therapeutic consideration of redemption and salvation, there flows a very challenging idea and ideal about health and healing. This could be easily misunderstood if one were to look merely at one's rights and duties. Those who speak of and partake in "health delivery" should examine the definition of health provided by the World Health Organization. They describe health as "a state of perfect physical, psychic and social well-being, and not only freedom from illness and ailment." We have to admire the efforts of this organization to widen the horizons of health and to propose Utopian ideals in an effort to promote good health measures.

Our own vision of health and wholeness is even more challenging. It includes, especially, the spiritual dimension, emphasizes healthy relationships and the constant need and effort to heal the civic community. At the same time, our point of departure and the whole approach are more realistic. We start by considering the undeniable fact of weakness and illness which will never be fully overcome. We call for solidarity in order to avoid the really avoidable evils, sufferings, and diseases and to concentrate on what can be healed.

Here, then, we face a wide range of challenges. We must uncover the deep meaning that can be given to suffering, especially that part of illness which resists our shared efforts of healing. The faith community surely does not need to confine itself to discussing ''why'' sickness and evil exist nor even ''how'' to master them. But the shared effort of waging war against sickness and suffering has to go hand in hand with uncovering and giving meaning to what cannot be healed. It is my deep conviction that in this way the realm of what can be healed will be astonishingly enlarged, and what cannot be actually healed will be freed from its worst viruses: meaninglessness and rebellion. An ongoing appreciation of compassion and loving care and a realization of the meaning of the highest values are continuing healing events.

In a fallen yet redeemed world, a true and fully human understanding of health implies a high degree of readiness to sacrifice and to suffer in active compassion or in meaningful acceptance of suffering, while all appropriate efforts of healing and of preventing illness are made.

Our model is Christ. He did not seek suffering as such nor did he seek unnecessary suffering; but he accepted all the suffering needed for our redemption, bearing the burden of all of us. So, too, in the therapeutic activity of the Church and in her compassion and shared suffering for the sake of healing and salvation, there is a privileged place for encouraging in ourselves and others a patient and meaningful acceptance of suffering that cannot be healed. This is part of the solidaric commitment to heal and to contend against evil conditions and illnesses, especially those caused by irresponsibility or some kind of abuse.

In the war against contagious diseases and also in the difficult struggle against the great "pestilences" of our modern time, such as alcoholism, drug addiction, and the many diseases arising from irresponsible life-styles, the Church can and must follow the example of Christ. He liberated the lepers and whole groups of people from degrading censure and alienation. The Church must do everything in her power to set energies free for healing and rehabilitation while contending against a loveless do-nothingism and a damaging judgmental attitude toward the different categories of sick people. While it is essential to warn against irresponsibility, so that suffering will be prevented as much as possible by constructive education, the warning must be wholly free from a judgmental attitude which would impugn the character of the sick person. The Church's attitude must always be geared to therapeutic, loving liberation.

While traveling around the leper colonies in Africa, I saw that among the Bantu tribes lepers go through exactly the same kind of psychic-social suffering as the lepers in Jesus' time. It is thought that they are being punished by God or by the spirits for their own faults. They are outcast and despised. But under the loving care of our Sisters and their helpers, the patients suddenly perceive themselves as living, loved, and lovable people. They discover that they are persons in the full sense, a dignified part of the Body of Christ. But then this affirmation comes to a sudden end. When the lepers are cured they cannot return to their families because, just as in old Israel and in many other cultures, leprosy has dissolved their marriages just as death does. They are also not able — especially in their cultural context — to live as single persons. But if ex-lepers then marry each other, they are excluded from the sacraments. Compassionate pastors tell them: "Don't worry too much, for Jesus loves you beyond the sacramental system." They weep with them in compassion and tell them: "I, too, do not fully understand the Church's law in this matter." Yet, I heard others say: "Why should we grant them the Eucharist? They are living in sin. The law is the law." It was consoling for me when I saw an African bishop react to those words, weeping like a child or, rather, like a mother weeps for her child.

In the fight against leprosy, which from a medical point of view can be cured, the realization has developed that in the struggle against this terrible disease the most important dimensions are social, cultural, psychological, and, above all, religious-spiritual. The encouraging approach of "community-medicine" does not neglect these dimensions. The Church must begin to tell people, not just by word but by a manifold action: "Leprosy is not at all a punishment by the gods. Leprosy is what people have made of it and still make of it. This epidemic will one day be only a humbling remembrance."

Our search for life's final meaning

Logotherapy, as proposed and developed by Viktor Frankl and his school, is a dimension of professional healing activity which richly resembles pastoral healing and redeeming ministry. Many have come to appreciate one of the basic insights of logotherapy that health has much to do with discovering the deep meaning of life and giving meaning to life through creative activity, harmonious social relationships, and by giving meaning finally to suffering. Healing happens, above all, through discovering and realizing its meaning in a fully human way.

It should be obvious that one's worst suffering is caused by a senseless life that has lost even the basic impulse to search for genuine meaning and refuses to enrich one's own and others' lives by authentic values. To give up the search for authentic values and meaning damages psychic and even somatic health; it destroys, or makes impossible, profound human relationships. Those who ease into this kind of insensitivity contaminate the whole environment in its spiritual-humanistic dimensions. They also are at least partly responsible for all modern forms of pollution, but especially cultural pollution. Such a senseless way of life spells imprisonment, enslavement, enmity to the very freedom which Christ has gained for us.

The best place to search for and attain this meaning is in a community of people who care for each other, mean much to each other, live conscientiously, and accept co-responsibility. Loss of meaning or of search for meaning can arise from a lack of community insight, of affirmation.

Many people go to the doctor or therapist without being organically ill. They are unable to tell what is wrong with them. They feel alienated, lost, depressed, without orientation in life. Often, too, somatic symptoms are present. Behind this phenomenon there is often the loss of a value system, frustrating purposelessness, a vaguely defined disappointment. They have no one who means much to them; they have lost their self-esteem, feel unloved, unappreciated, and unlistened to by those who could give sympathy. They feel socially dead, and because of this they sometimes attempt suicide — which frequently is their last desperate cry for loving attention.

Every practitioner should know about these aspects and be ready to give some help, some encouragement in people's search to give meaning to life. In many cases, however, the preferred response would be a referral to a logotherapist or to a pastor who is competent in these matters. This very real vacuum — the loss of meaning and lack of a value system — is due to social isolation and gravely disturbed human relationships; and all psychotherapeutic efforts normally will fail in this area unless the social context and community relationships are taken into consideration.

In logotherapy, special effort should be made to lead to a sense of community, to integration into helpful groups, and to personal interrelationships that can become wholesome and helpful in the search for meaning. Since doctor and patient join in the ongoing search for the deeper meaning of life, the patient soon becomes aware that he or she not only should seek and accept help, through contact with a healing community and dependable persons, but also should begin to support others and the community in this ongoing journey.

Very frequently in my experience, a psychotherapist has suggested at a certain point that the patient should see me or another priest to talk more explicitly on the spiritual dimension of the person's neurosis or to seek improvement through the celebration of the healing sacrament of Reconciliation. On such an occasion, if possible, the priest should draw the person's attention to a zealous group or community which can give support.

From both a pastoral and a therapeutic point of view, pastoral counseling and private confession, with total neglect of community spirit and community-building, is dangerously one-sided. Personal confession together with communal celebration of reconciliation and healing should constantly foster the reconciled and reconciling community. Those who proclaim salvation in all its forms should be alert for the many opportunities which — by shared faith and the Word of God — become a grace-filled opportunity in the search for meaning by those who are wavering and those threatened by loss of meaning and value appreciation.

The healing mission of the Church and the concerns of logotherapy are not adequately taken care of by those who speak only in general and somehow abstract terms of ultimate meaning. The person must be helped to search for meaning and authentic values in an existential way, in the concrete context of his or her life. In this search, those who feel oppressed by the fragility and futility of life and are angry about corrupt conditions — while not yet being able or perhaps not yet even trying to face their mortality — need more than theoretical responses. They need encouragement and support in order to conquer the crises of suffering in a meaningful way.

Authentic help in the formation of an upright *conscience* is one of the best ways to carry out Christ's mandate to heal people. Here much can be learned from the principles and wisdom of logotherapy. A Christian approach to formation of conscience will give marked attention to the primacy of grace and to the insights provided by experience. Ill-timed imperatives should never conceal the "law of grace."

Frankl rightly alerts the logotherapist never to try to impose his or her own convictions — especially in an authoritarian manner — on one who wants to set out on his or her own search for meaning. Imposition easily becomes full-fledged manipulation which impedes people in their personal search for truth and meaning. Logotherapy encourages people to dare the journey of ongoing search for ever-deeper meaning, in openness to the Thou and We and in readiness to receive witness and light from people whose lives vouch for fullness of meaning.

This implies that the pastoral counselor as well as the secular logotherapist will clearly concede to the other person the right to doubt and to spell out his or her doubts. Even in matters of faith and morality there is need of a healthy way to face doubts honestly instead of looking for easy assurances. Of course, we have to discern between doubts, as intrinsic part of the search for truth and meaning, and superficial skepticism or frivolous suspicions that often arise from refusal to put truth and meaning into practice. I feel strongly that we have to give greater respect and attention to healthy doubts in an honest search for life's meaning. Courteous dialogue is the opposite of indifferentism and far more fruitful for both parties than arrogance and intolerance.

The Second Vatican Council's Declaration on Religious Freedom, if seen in this perspective, throws more light on the scope and meaning of therapeutics. It entails freedom to search honestly for truth — while respecting the conscience of each individual — in deference to those who are on their way toward more light.

For a therapeutic moral theology, the elucidation of value and meaning is an indispensable presupposition for the liberating and healing teaching about norms and laws. Similarly, sound pastoral practice will never try to impose, by threats or manipulation, a law or an imperative which, here and now, cannot be honestly assimilated by the person. It is not a matter of theoretical ignorance but of an existential impossibility. This was one of the strong points in the pastoral theology of Saint Alphonsus de Liguori.

We distinguish between the individual judgment of conscience and conscience as a gift of nature. Judgment can be erroneous; conscience itself can become sick. Logotherapy works for the healing of a sick conscience. A conscience is sick:

(1) when it has lost its inner dynamics to search seriously for what is true and good — its search for meaning. The cause may be parents, pastors, or other educators who look just for security and submission, thus restricting the thirst for meaning.

(2) when it insists on law without discerning the underlying values, without asking first for meaning.

(3) when, through long and unrepented sinfulness, it has gradually destroyed its inborn dynamic toward ''realizing truth'' or, more specifically, ''realizing truth in love.''

(4) when it lacks reverence or openness for the conscience of others — because it no longer respects the conscience of each individual.

We act in a logotherapeutic and pastoral way by discerning and unmasking the forms of sickness in the individual conscience so that we may patiently assist the person on the road to healing.

Specifically Christian, pastoral logotherapy leads the searcher-for-meaning to Christ, who is the Logos and Therapist, the Truth, the Life, the Way to truth and life.

Bernard Tyrrell chose the word "Christotherapy" as the title for one of his books. His meaning is clear: it is a respectful, gentle guide leading the conscience itself to open to Christ, the healing Light. And it is the task of the whole community of salvation and of each member according to his or her special charism to point the way to Christ by healing love. Logotherapy, like Christotherapy, happens when the dynamics of faith-witness are experienced through solidarity and respect for the conscience of each individual. Thus the community becomes the organ of Christ.

Such proclamation of salvation and logotherapeutic pastoral life also respectfully accepts everything that is truly meaningful for the individual and community in non-Christian religions and alien cultures; for these, too, are seeds of the Logos.

Genuine Christotherapy is an ongoing process of conversion and growth in the context of communities which are constantly on the road of renewal, clearly directed toward Christ and his reign of love and peace, indeed guided by Christ himself in ever-deepening solidarity. Christotherapy needs the cooperation of the whole community — of pastors, charismatic loving people, and, last but not least, professionally qualified logotherapists.

Chapter Five

FAITH THAT HEALS AND SETS US FREE

Through the community of salvation and, especially, through holy charismatic members of the community, Christ, the divine-human Healer, awakens the "inner physician" who dwells and works within us through faith. It is through faith that we open ourselves to the healing power of Christ.

In this context, we speak of that faith which becomes part of our whole being, persuading us to fashion ourselves after Christ, to make our fundamental option for him, and to embrace "sound doctrine" which will light our way to "realizing the truth in love" and knowing Christ and the Father even better. This is the faith which we celebrate joyously in the sacraments of faith and through which we entrust ourselves to God: a faith that bears fruit in love and justice and articulates and manifests itself in many signs of salvation and peace. It comes to its full embodiment in all the virtues, especially in the eschatological virtues so greatly praised by the Bible.

Healing power of faith

On several occasions Jesus speaks explicitly of the connection between his healing power and the faith of the people he heals. To the blind man who entreats him, "I want my sight back," Jesus responds, "Go; your faith has cured you" (Mark 10:52; cf. Matthew 9:22; Luke 7:50). By faith one opens oneself to the saving and healing power that comes from God and touches the innermost being, as if a doctor were dwelling there.

In order to unfold its healing and saving power, faith must be "healthy," able to respond joyfully and wholeheartedly to the love with which Jesus — the Emmanuel, "God-with-us" — meets us; it must also be able to respond to "sound doctrine" that does not stray into sterile theory or dispute "about mere words" (see 2 Timothy 2:14). The faith that heals us welcomes God's life-giving word as the greatest gift and as a call to give ourselves as gift in heartfelt gratitude.

Faith has the power to free us from guilt and anguish and to fill us with trust in God's healing forgiveness. If we wish to retain this power, we should never harbor a false, narrow image of God as a revengeful judge. As Christians we have only one genuine image of God: Jesus Christ and, in union with him, those who are authentic images of Christ. In healing faith we adore and "know" intimately Christ, our Savior, the merciful Samaritan who has come not to condemn but to save and heal us.

A healing, saving faith does not mean that we are guiltless. Rather, this faith gives us the humble courage to confess our sins, to lay open our hearts with all their wounds to the Divine Physician. "If we confess our sins, he is just, and may be trusted to forgive our sins and cleanse us from every kind of wrong" (1 John 1:9). "Even if our conscience condemns us, God is greater than our conscience and knows all" (1 John 3:20). We can experience fully the saving and healing power of faith only if, while confessing our sins, we praise God's saving justice and mercy and firmly believe the supreme truth that "God is Love" for all who seek him with a sincere heart. This does not mean that our love must be already perfect but, rather, that we recognize the need of further purification and conversion and keep striving for these day by day, moment by moment. In this way the process of healing will produce manifold results.

An eminent result and sign of the ongoing healing process is one's inner peace and the capacity to radiate peace and serenity. Miraculous forces overflow, then, from one's spiritual center into the psychosomatic areas; healing becomes all-embracing and, at the same time, a sign of salvation.

It cannot be overemphasized that we do not attribute the healing power to a momentary, transitory feeling of faith but, rather, to the "virtue of faith," as classical theology called it: that faith by which we devotedly follow Christ, remain close to him, and grow in knowledge and love of Jesus and the Father. So, the process of faith is a continuing and concurrent event of both salvation and healing.

We can express the same truth by the term "faith conversion." Through faith in God and Jesus Christ, we make a radical fundamental option which strives for and produces a persistent deepening, an "ongoing conversion," as the Church Fathers express it. Yet, this fundamental option can be in great danger of being aborted unless it unfolds and engraves itself ever more in our striving, yearning, thinking, and in our conduct.

Believers, who in peace and joy have experienced the saving and healing powers of faith, proclaim salvation and participate in the healing power of Christ in a way that leads others gently to Christ, the Healer. This happens constantly, for instance, with AA members who praise God openly for his healing, thus inspiring new hope and trust even in those who have been considered "hopeless cases." William James once observed that more alcoholics have been cured by religious conversion than by all the medicine in the world. And, despite the advances of modern psychiatry, I agree with J. Kovel who, in *A Complete Guide to Therapy,* suspects the same observation would be true today.

In view of the very substance of faith, its saving-healing power, and our understanding of genuine human health, it must be repeated that we are speaking of faith in a faith community, in salvation solidarity. We can hardly expect that a faith conversion, even one initially genuine, can be kept preserved and deepened without support of a lively faith community and its communal determination to give thanks for support by making it an ever more healing community. Thus, believers on the way to salvation and healing are liberated from isolation and estrangement. They sense ever more clearly the closeness of the Emmanuel — "God with us." It should never be forgotten that worship — a genuine prayer life in a faith community and personal prayer — is the life breath of saving and healing faith.

Theology, too, as E. Bieser writes, can fulfill its therapeutic function and dimension only when it has its roots in a prayerful faith community. If it deteriorates into a merely intellectual operation on the level of scientific endeavor, it will be more an obstacle than a help for the healing and saving power of faith.

Christian faith cannot be thought of without adoration, whereby we recognize God gratefully as the source and goal of life and praise him for the gift of revelation and salvation. By adoration "in Spirit and truth," humankind finds its wholeness and center. Believers arrive at their own truth, healed from deception and confusion. This is part of the process of salvation but equally of ongoing healing through faith. Freed from paganistic and dangerous ideologies, believers find the way of salvation and the courage and strength to overcome destructive conduct and harmful relationships. "Those who are real worshippers will worship the Father in spirit and in truth. Such are the worshippers whom the Father wants." They shall draw water from "an inner spring always welling up for eternal life" (John 4:23-24, 4:14).

Healing power of trust in God

An extremely dangerous suffering, which psychotherapists and pastors meet frequently and which sometimes withstands all healing efforts, is an overwhelmingly oppressive *anxiety*. It has deep and wide-ranging ramifications with devastating psychosomatic consequences, and should be carefully distinguished from the fear one faces in a concrete danger. Sometimes it is caused by a loss of meaning in life and a collapse of one's value system, but most frequently it arises from a false, threatening image of God that shapes the whole world about us. What today we call "anxiety neurosis," moralists, since the seventeenth century, call "scrupulosity." The afflicted person is not just tormented by doubts about whether this or that is sin or even mortal sin — although this, too, may be a part of suffering. What is more characteristic is an all-pervading anxiety about being guilty and worthy of punishment, distress about failing life's purpose in spite of all good will.

In the religious history of humankind, people have suffered terribly from anxiety about a vengeful God, vengeful spirits, a cruel fate persecuting them. The apostle of the Gentiles depicts the torment of people who seek in vain for justice by "keeping the laws" and imposing all kinds of laws on others because they do not know or do not accept by faith the healing-saving justice coming from a compassionate God through the Savior.

Not every feeling of anxiety of itself is pathological. Heidegger describes human existence as "being-destined-to-death," and this is sometimes manifested in a tortured feeling, especially if the thought of one's own mortality is stubbornly repressed. If, on the contrary, the person reaches the freedom to face his or her death in an enlightened and meaningful way, multiple energies for health and creativity can be set free through a genuine "reconciliation" with the prospect of death.

Both the therapist and the pastor meet people troubled by a deep anxiety that sometimes breaks through in time of illness, when they experience insecurity and an enormous threat to their existence. This anxiety often can be traced back to childhood experiences of rejection, which have been reactivated by a legalistic religion wherein "the law" matters more than people. This happens more easily to people who are endowed with a deep religiosity. They yearn to know the God of love but are often confronted with religious authorities who rigorously inculcate legal or ethical imperatives, which make little or no sense to them and cannot be fulfilled without great risks to their basic human relationships.

At various times in my pastoral and theological experience I have been flooded with letters and visits from people who found themselves at the edge of despair and rebellion for such reasons. Reading the Gospel against the background of similar experiences, I really appreciate Bernhard Hanssler's words about anxiety and hope: "The therapy against anguish which comes from Jesus is immeasurable in its psycho-hygienic dynamics. The study of history of religions and comparative study of religions give all evidence that Jesus, among all founders of religion, is unique also insofar as he has removed from religion the anguishing elements."

As the Emmanuel, "God-with-us," Jesus heals tortured people

by his loving presence, by his loving affirmation. Teaching us to call God his Father, with the same loving and trusting word which he used, "Abba," he shows us the Father. Sinners and outcasts feel restored by him to dignity and trust. And this should be seen as a basic rule for the Church to which Jesus has entrusted the continuation of his healing ministry.

If God would allow me to ask for one charism, I would not hesitate to ask for the great, loving art of freeing anxious people from this terrible plague. I have no such miraculous power nor do countless others. But what we can do, each in his or her own field, is to remain faithful to Jesus by preventing anxiety as much as possible and healing people from anxiety wherever we can. Let us put a stop to the cruelty that arises from unsound teaching and unhealthy pastoral practice. Moral theologians, especially, must be constantly on the alert to make certain that their teachings convey the liberating message of the "law of grace" and show the healing countenance of the Savior.

Laws and moral imperatives must never be separated from the insights provided by divine goodness and graciousness. Those norms, which in the complexity of life often give rise to severe conflicts with other crucial values and norms, must be open to interpretation. We should be willing to learn something from the use of *oikonomia* (the therapeutic application of norms and exceptions) of the Oriental churches and our own best tradition about *epikeia* (justice according to natural law or right). Our guiding question should always be: "What kind of image of God do we convey? Is it that image, that countenance of the loving Father, that Jesus has shown us?"

Whenever Jesus told sick persons that they were healed "by faith," it is evident that they had great trust and confidence in him and, through him, trust in the heavenly Father. It was Jesus who awakened and strengthened it. In his person and by his deeds he invited them to trust and be liberated from anxiety and doubt. The sick perceived him as the fulfillment of God's promises and assurance of even greater chances of salvation, liberation, and healing.

Believers are on the road to salvation and healing when they entrust themselves in everything to the Lord, confident that God can turn to our good whatever comes to pass. This kind of trust was expressed by the last words written by Dietrich Bonhoeffer on the very morning of his execution:

> Sheltered wonderfully by powers of goodness,
> trustfully we await whatever may happen.
> God is with us at evening and morningtide,
> and surely on every new day.

The new relationship of the redeemed person with the Giver of life and of all good things leads to meaningful trust in personal relationships and also becomes a source of trust for others, a mirror image of trust in God. At the same time our inner physician, dwelling and working within us, directs our attention to the Spirit who renews the world and the heart of humankind.

Trust in Jesus gives an abiding hope while also freeing us from false hopes and misleading aspirations. The One who bore the burden of our sins on the Cross and prepared us for healing through his own wounds helps us also, day by day, to accept our cross and the mandate to bear each other's burdens. By entrusting ourselves to the Lord, we will experience what he meant when he said: "Come to me, all whose work is hard, whose load is heavy; and I will give you relief" (Matthew 11:28). Hope-filled trust and joy in the Lord give us ever new vigor and help us discover new fountains of health and healing in the depths of our being.

A constantly recurring theme in the Acts of the Apostles and the Letters of Paul is that the disciples of Christ and heralds of the Good News can bring consolation and encouragement to their fellow Christians even in the midst of trial and suffering, if they have entrusted themselves completely to the Lord. Those who have suffered with Christ become more able and willing to make their own the sufferings of others; their own compassion and their readiness to make whatever sacrifices are required by active, healing love make this possible. By working together, we all can transform suffering, give it a new meaning. In this way we can heal what can be healed and bear the rest in Christian hope.

Healing power of redeemed love

Those whose love is egocentric are themselves sick; and, as they become ever more so, the more sickening they become to others. But an outgoing love, coming from God and leading to God, makes real sense and guarantees a blessed future. Redeemed and redeeming-healing love is a most precious fruit of faith. Jesus healed people, above all, through his love. This love awakened faith and trust in him. Martin Deutinger, a great moral theologian of the last century, was so right when he wrote, ''Only love can do wonders.''

Redeemed and redeeming love can mobilize our deepest healing powers. It reveals to us the true meaning and purpose of all the treasures of God's kingdom. This love is the heart of the proclamation of salvation, pointing and leading to the final celebration of love in the communion of saints, where salvation, beatitude, and human wholeness will blend together.

One cannot praise too highly the therapeutic power of redeemed love, for this is an essential dimension of salvation and redemption. Care must be taken, however, that we speak of the right kind of love. To gain this essential knowledge, Holy Scripture gives us clear criteria in 1 Corinthians 13 and Galatians 5, where Paul writes about Jesus' love, which is the source and model of redeeming love. And we would add that, for us and for our witness, the healing power of personal relationships, the discovery of our own and others' inner healing resources, and joint efforts for the healing of the civic community are among the most striking and encouraging signs of genuine love.

"There is nothing love cannot face; there is no limit to its faith, its hope, and its endurance" (1 Corinthians 13:7). By engracing our hearts with his love, God favors us highly. This same love gives us the power to grant to others, time and again, some of our own goodness and trust. And this in itself constitutes a healing power.

Healing power of certain biblical virtues

As we have seen, faith and love manifest the saving and healing presence of the kingdom of God. They are signs of the "end times." They give form and strength to all the other virtues.

Here we are not concerned with the four "cardinal virtues" which the Church adopted and adapted from the Hellenistic culture. Rather, we wish to consider those biblical virtues which, besides faith, hope, and love and as manifestation of them, make us active participants in the history of salvation and thus also in the history of healing. We will appraise these virtues in accord with the three dimensions of history: past, present, and future.

• *Gratitude (for the past)*

Our most basic gift, according to Saint Alphonsus, is our *memory*; without it our intellect and will would have nothing to work with. Memory makes us active participants in history. It allows the riches of the past to become operative in the present. It provides and calls for coherence and fidelity.

Through a *grateful memory,* all that God has done up till now, all the marvelous achievements of humankind in the past, and all that is precious in traditions can be revitalized. The past influences us by offering us the fruits of its own experience. Our own inner value and strength depend to a great extent on a grateful memory. This biblical virtue enables us to celebrate meaningfully and live faithfully the *Eucharist,* which means *thanksgiving.* A grateful memory makes us willing and able to share what we have received in the past and from the past. We not only draw lessons from it, we activate it, revitalize it, and direct it to new fields of operation.

The importance of gratitude — understood as *grateful memory* — becomes more evident when we think of the opposite: a poor, sick memory beset by resentment, discontent, and animosity, which impoverish the individual and the community. Even worse, the sick memory is destructive. It copies only the worst of the past. Constantly, it reopens and magnifies old wounds. The ungrateful have nothing to contribute to the present hour. They waste time in lamentation and accusation. Because of their dissatisfaction, they are not free to appreciate others or even themselves in a healthy way.

Grateful persons are gracious sharers, never condescending, for they know that what they share has been given to them and can remain a precious gift only when gratefully shared. Thankful people are not only attentive to all the good they have inherited from the past; they are also alert to others, to free them gradually from their self-destructive hostilities. One of the greatest achievements in healing is the healing of wounded memories. A community of grateful believers, a truly "Eucharistic community," is a fountain of health and healing.

● *Vigilance, readiness, and discernment*
  (for the present)

Gratitude builds on and is shaped by those biblical virtues which open the eyes of believers to the present opportunities, the present moment (*kairos*), this hour of salvation (*hora*). The virtues that enable us to grasp the offering of the present moment are: *vigilance, readiness, discernment*. We cannot live healthily in the presence of the Lord of history without keen appreciation of every moment that invites us to act with him in the history of salvation and healing.

The Lord and his apostles — in many parables and manifold warnings — show us the importance of *vigilance:* watchfulness for the Lord's coming. If we live in his presence, always ready to see what the present moment requires from us, our whole life becomes this prayer: "Lord, here I am, call me! Send me!" Thus we shall be prepared for his final coming when he arrives to call us home in the hour of our death.

Readiness is a direct result of gratitude and vigilance. It is a sign of our conformity with the will of God, as well as a criterion for discernment. This attitude of readiness prevents us from mere daydreaming about generalities. It prepares us for the gift of discernment by helping us to discover the existential meaning of "this hour" in the service of the kingdom of God.

Discernment asks: "What, here and now, should be my acceptable contribution to the ongoing history of salvation, liberation, and healing?" Those who are open to all the dimensions of history will find the best answers by asking these questions: What, now, is the best possible expression of my gratitude? What is the next step toward the future? What can I render to the Lord for what he has done for me, and how can I serve those who are my companions on the journey of salvation history?

Any desire, word, or deed that would deprive us of serenity and peace of mind will deprive us of the solution to our here-and-now situation. Discernment reminds us to first summon our inner peace. Then we can deal with grave problems and make daring decisions.

To better understand the healthy and healing quality of the virtues of people who live the present moment, we look again to their opposites, to those sterile "unhealthy" people who seem to live constantly on the edge of the "if only": "If only this or that were different, what wonders I could do!" Unhappy, estranged, they always fail to perceive the present hour.

● *Hope (for the future)*

Our Christian future is illumined by *hope* based on the divine promises. Hope, in the fullest sense, offers a genuine goal. The supporting virtues are responsibility for the near future — a future of peace, justice, wholesome public life — and responsibility to pass on to new generations a healthy social and ecological environment.

Eschatological hope allows us to seek ideal perfection as we probe for better ways to ensure peace — as an example — for future generations. This is what underlies *discernment,* where all the eschatological virtues play a role. We must never pursue ideals which betray the *present* (the presence of the moment and the immediate presence of God and of people) as the Marxist Utopians do. To do that would be to contradict the final hope of humankind.

Sick persons who have helpers and friends marked by these biblical virtues will be able to impart meaning to their lives, discover their own inner powers, and, above all, make use of the positive opportunities provided for them. Christian hope and all the other virtues described here are characterized by the light and direction they give when we are faced with suffering and disappointment.

The eschatological virtues imply that we are on the road with Christ who is the Way, the Truth, and the Life. And, joined with him as his disciples, we travel on our way in Christian solidarity.

Healing powers of the sacraments

As we have seen, the biblical virtues introduce us actively into the history of salvation and healing. All this, of course, happens through grace. The sacraments of salvation are channels of God's saving and healing grace. They teach and enable us to become both receptive and creative for salvation history.

Christ is the origin and center of all the sacraments, which thus become effective signs of salvation. In him and through him the Church is to be and to become ever more an all-embracing efficacious sign (sacrament). Her first mission is not "to do" but "to *be*," so that through her very being, her true face (the saving-healing love of Christ) shines through, thus becoming visible and accessible to faith experience. Her saving-healing teaching depends on how much the Church as a whole, each Church community and each of her members, becomes a kind of sacrament, an appealing, energizing sign of redeemed and re-deeming, saving and healing love.

The seven sacraments of the Church and all the other signs and symbols of salvation are directed to the continuing event of salvation history. If we want to understand more fully how this proclamation-celebration of the mystery of salvation blends with the healing ministry, it is necessary to give more attention to this vision of sacramentality and faith witness. It is a disheartening fact that, during past centuries, moral theologians and catechism writers treated the sacraments only *after* the commandments and with a very legalistic approach to life. Because of this, many Catholics did not fully understand the healing power of the sacra-ments and of the Church at large.

● *Baptism*

Bible, tradition, and liturgy teach us that through Baptism we take part in a new creation. By means of grace, faith, and the effective signs of faith, Baptism places us in a new saving relationship with God, Father of all, with Christ, Savior of all, and with the Holy Spirit who renews the face of the earth and the hearts of the People of God. As a consequence, there also arise new saving-healing-liberating relationships with all the redeemed, with the world redeemed by Christ, with culture, society, and the earth itself. The more substantial these relationships are, the more will the baptized live the gift and mission bestowed on them in Baptism.

The sacrament of Baptism inserts us into the history of salvation, but its reception is more than just a beginning. Rather, it is a continuing experience, a divine assurance of our commitment to live and to grow ever more steadfastly in accord with this sacrament of faith, salvation, and healing.

● *Confirmation*

Confirmation opens our hearts and directs our attention to the "Spirit of Truth" who, from within, teaches us sincere love, enables us to live a life in truth, leads us to authentic maturity, strengthens us on the road to full responsibility, and protects our psychic and spiritual life from crippling selfishness, both individual and collective. As Christians, we know that the "Spirit of Truth" is the real source of *satyagraha,* "the strength of truth in love" in us, as Gandhi defines it.

Confirmation signifies the abiding gift of strength which will enable us to embrace gratefully and courageously our mission and responsibility for the healthiness of the public sphere of life. Confirmed believers can and must be fully aware that their own salvation and their wholeness-identity-integrity depend very much on how faithfully they carry out their commitment to the Savior of the world. This entails responsibility to work — together with all people of good will — for wholesome civic convictions, a more mature and balanced culture, economy, and political life. In this way we will begin to build a more just, more peaceful, and healthier world.

• *Eucharist*

In Christ and in the Church, Eucharist is the central and most fruitful sacrament of the saving-healing grace of God. It is also a principal sign of "forgiveness of sins," of healing hurt memories, a source of peace, and a powerful means for encouraging the peace mission of all Christians. Eucharist is an efficacious sign of healing faith, hope, and love that enables the community and each believer to radiate wholeness and peace, to serve the poor, to care for the sick, and to heal the depressed and anguished. When duly celebrated, it communicates ever anew that joy in the Lord which is a main source of strength and health.

The Eucharist is a memorial celebration through which we meet Christ in grateful remembrance of how he reached out for the exiled and the sick while proclaiming the Good News. Through a grateful memory we live in the presence of Christ and experience, in faith, how he identified and still identifies himself with our sufferings and with a sick humanity. When, in this memorial, we praise him for having borne our burden, he engraves in our hearts and memories his mandate to bear a part of the burden of others, especially of the sick. Thus, we participate in his caring-healing ministry.

Just as in Christ's earthly mission the proclamation of salvation was firmly united with his healing activity, so in the Eucharistic memorial the faith experience of Jesus' sacrificial love cannot be separated from the call of the needy, suffering, and sick, through whom Christ turns to us and tests our faith.

The saving word of Jesus in the Eucharist, "Do this in memory of me," reminds us gently but inexorably of the anticipated Final Judgment: "You have visited me when I was sick . . . whatever you have done to the least of my brethren, you have done to me."

These words urge us to make a clear choice both for Christ and for the suffering members of his Body. How could we truthfully say our "Amen" to the words "This is my body" if we would refuse to say "Yes, here I am" when Christ's Body cries out in its suffering for love, care, and help?

When we receive the body of Christ we are always confronted with his question as to whether we want to be and act as mutually responsible members of the Body of Christ. A truly Eucharistic, grateful memory will help us to say our responsible "Amen" when the need of others appeals to our active love. The creative, healing, caring solidarity of the Christian community with the sick and suffering is an integral dimension of the Eucharistic memorial and of a faith-filled memory bearing fruit in caring, healing love.

The Eucharistic ministry, by which Communion is brought to the aged, disabled, and sick, is thoroughly consistent only to the extent that the whole Eucharistic community participates in the caring-healing assistance which is given according to the charisms and capabilities of its members. At the same time, we should remember that the sick and their families, who have their share in the suffering, are thus drawn into the invitation "Do this in memory of me," which is an appeal to be and to become ever more active members of Christ's Body. Their creative suffering and the family's loving care can enter effectively into the total mission of the Church to heal and to reveal, to suffer and to heal. Their loyal "Amen," renewed day by day, becomes a continuing gift to the Body of Christ. For themselves and for others, this has a saving-healing power. Their suffering and caring, united with the Eucharistic-healing community, have a bearing on the salvation, wholeness, and health of all.

Any effort toward a faithful fulfillment of the twofold yet unified mission to proclaim the Good News and to heal and to be lovingly present to the suffering cannot ignore these dimensions of the Eucharist and a Eucharistic spirituality.

• Penance (Reconciliation)

To proclaim the Gospel and to heal, it is vitally important for the Church to see the sacraments which bring forgiveness of sins in a clear relationship with her healing ministry. In a true spirit of ecumenism we can learn much from the Orthodox churches. They always saw the mystery of redemption, as well as the sacraments of forgiveness, in the light of healing. I say the "sacraments" because, for the Oriental Christians just as for the Western (Latin) Church of ancient time, the Eucharist has always been seen as a *therapeutic* event of forgiveness of sins and the granting of peace: "This is the cup of my blood . . . for the forgiveness of sins." The specific sacrament of Reconciliation (called in the West, "Penance" or "confession") was seen explicitly as empowered by the Eucharist and directed toward it.

In the West the sacrament of Penance came to reflect the theory of redemption prevailing since Saint Anselm, who saw it chiefly as reparation required by a vindictive justice. So, Penance and, later, the painfully precise confession conceived as punishment-reparation (receiving its merits from the reparation wrought by Christ) lost their emphasis on therapy. This thought pattern was also a reflection of a vindictive-justice pattern of that culture. Meanwhile, in the Eastern Church the ordinary confession (to be distinguished from the rehabilitation processes after gravely criminal or gravely scandalous sins) was thoroughly understood in the light of Christ's word: "I have come to heal sinners."

It has to be noted, however, that even in the West the therapeutic emphasis has found supporters from time to time. Outstanding in his support is Saint Alphonsus. With great courage he withstood the tide. In one of his books written especially for confessors he explains their ministry: "In the *first* place, the confessor must be a father" — one who, by his loving kindness and compassion, "makes visible the heavenly Father." Prime attention should be given to Jesus' words: "Be compassionate as your Father is compassionate" (Luke 6:36).

"In the *second* place, the confessor must be a healer" — one who portrays and shares in Christ's mission as Healer. This is possible only if the confessor has previously helped the penitent to experience the compassion of the heavenly Father.

"In the *third* place," the confessor must be a "teacher of the law," which is "the law of Christ," a law of love and saving-healing solidarity. He is expected to teach "sound doctrine." He may never enforce man-made traditions or beliefs to the detriment of the all-embracing vision of love of God and neighbor. And, above all, he must respect the penitent's sincere conscience, even if he (the confessor) thinks he has good reasons to consider it erroneous. He may never manipulate anyone's conscience but, rather, will help the person, in the light of Jesus, to search for what is true, good, beautiful, and healing.

"And in the fourth and *last* place, he must act as judge." Seen in the full light of the other main dimensions, the ministry of judge includes nothing that would threaten the penitent or cause anxiety. On the contrary, it implies guidance toward the vision of God's saving justice, to a sense of discernment, and to a readiness to make amends, especially when it is a matter of healing wounds inflicted on others or repairing as far as possible the damage done by scandal. This is often indispensable for the penitent's own healing, wholeness, and authenticity.

My belief is that the present crisis of the sacrament of Penance could be overcome if it were better understood as a sacrament that truly integrates *reconciliation and peace*. This applies as much to the individual confession as to the communal celebration of this sacrament. The two forms do not compete with each other; rather, they complete each other.

This understanding of the sacrament can also liberate people from an unhealthy obsession created by a simplistic distinction between "serious and venial sins" or "grave and only venial sins." This distinction becomes impossible in a therapeutic approach. Of course, "mortal sin" is most serious, just as senseless death is. But no doctor would call only death a "serious" or "grave" matter: he is faced with all conceivable degrees of gravity, and he knows that sometimes a lesser illness left untreated can develop into grave, very serious, extremely serious, and, finally, deadly illness.

A Christian who has this therapeutic understanding of the sacrament will not tell himself or herself, "My sins are not mortal. Therefore, I don't need the sacramental encounter with Christ, the Healer." Instead, out of respect for Christ the Healer and in his own interest, he will do his best — by earnest repentance, trust, serious endeavor, and through the grace of this sacrament of reconciliation and peace — to prevent his spiritual illness from developing into grave and, finally, mortal downfall.

● *Anointing of the Sick*

The saving-healing dimension of the sacrament called Anointing of the Sick is particularly evident both in Scripture and in liturgy.

In the West for many centuries the term *Extreme Unction* has clouded the therapeutic dimension by frightening people and discouraging them from timely reception. Now, Vatican Council II has restored the emphasis on healing. " 'Extreme Unction,' which may also and more fittingly be called 'Anointing of the Sick,' is not a sacrament only for those who are at the point of death. Hence, as soon as anyone of the faithful begins to be in danger of death from sickness or old age, the fitting time for him to receive this sacrament has certainly already arrived" (Liturgy, #73).

The biblical text frequently quoted in this context clearly looks to the blending of saving and healing power. "Is one of you ill? He should send for the elders of the congregation to pray over him and anoint him with oil in the name of the Lord. The prayer offered in faith will save the sick man, the Lord will raise him from his bed, and any sins he may have committed will be forgiven. Therefore confess your sins to one another, and pray for one another, and then you will be healed" (James 5:14-16).

The wording in the original Greek text suggests even more the relation between raising the sick from their bed and raising them to everlasting life, between healing and saving. This text also, like the various liturgical rites, emphasizes the community aspect of caring, healing, saving. It is heartening to see now in so many places all over the world loving and, indeed, healing community celebrations of the sacrament of Anointing of the Sick, sometimes in connection with the Eucharistic celebration. The way in which the parish community cooperates, concelebrates, and receives new inspirations for the care of the sick, the elderly, and the lonely is not the least of the blessings of this creative return to our oldest traditions.

In this way, too, we bring to light the role of our senior citizens ("elders" in the broad sense). Many of them have learned to visit the sick and, especially, the lonely, combining helpful acts with cheerful listening, conversation, comfort, and prayer. In the Anointing of the Sick, seen in connection with meaningful visitation, three things take place: *healing love, comforting faith,* and *redeeming-saving suffering.*

The purpose of the faithful is to help the ill person experience Christ's *healing love* for the sick, through the members' sharing and caring. The heartfelt love for the person is the result of faith in the redeeming, healing love of Jesus.

The sick person is *comforted and strengthened by the witness of faith* which speaks not just in words but in the total truth of life, sharing, and caring.

Thus, the suffering of the sick enters more fully into the light of Christ's *redeeming-saving suffering*. By discerning the deeper meaning of suffering its sting is lessened. Whatever can be healed will be healed; and the rest will be no longer meaningless, depressing suffering.

The sick believers are not just recipients. Accepting the sharing-caring love of others and their thoughtful witness of faith, they themselves become radiating, healing, saving centers of the tri-unity of love-faith-Christlike suffering. They are important partners in the saving-healing love and suffering of Christ, for the good of the whole Body of Christ.

The more the faith community learns to understand this blending of love, faith witness, and suffering, the more effectively and generously can the sick receive and return it. Thus, the sick and their families are much more than objects of pastoral care; they are frequently able to return more than they receive, in a mutual exchange of gifts.

● *Matrimony*

In the past the healing aspect of Matrimony has been mistakenly confined to the narrow perspective of the doctrine on the goals of marital intercourse (healing, quieting concupiscence). The true picture is far more beautiful. Spouses, parents, children, all members of the family are called to be and are enabled by grace to be for each other efficacious signs of God's saving-healing love, through their healthy and healing relationships. They should be fully conscious that they are graced fellow travelers on the road to maturity, wholeness, salvation, holiness.

Care must be taken that betrothed couples do not indulge in Utopian dreams. They should be ready to accept each other in their complex reality, with their inner strengths but also with their defects and wounds to be healed. The more they help each other in grateful mutual acceptance to discover their inner resources, the better they can deal with their mutual flaws.

For all members of a Christian family the words of Viktor Frankl are particularly meaningful: "Love is the best applied logotherapy." The unconditional mutual acceptance and the shared faith enable all to mature, to grow, to heal, and to be healed. By this kind of love they direct each other constantly to Christ, the Savior, Sanctifier, and Healer.

• *Ministerial Priesthood*

Through calling and sacrament, Christ, the Healer and Savior, establishes a new special relationship with those whom he has chosen to serve his people as deacon, priest, or bishop. Just as they are called to proclaim and celebrate the mystery of salvation, so are they also meant to embody, in Christ, the blend between revealing and healing in their ministry and, of course, like all of the faithful, in their lives.

They can best understand this mission as "wounded healers" touched by the Divine Physician. They must know that they are in need of the Savior and Healer, Jesus Christ, just as much as others; only the self-righteous exclude themselves from being healed and becoming healers in Christ. The priest does not need to don a mask to hide his wounds and his vulnerability. In the freedom of the sons of God, he can acknowledge his shortcomings and confess his sins, since he is grateful for being accepted and affirmed by the Divine Physician. And as he turns to his flock in sympathetic, healing love, he likewise needs the patient, healing acceptance on the part of all the faithful. The members of the ministerial priesthood are meant to serve in such a way that the whole community realizes the perfect blend between revealing and healing, which is open to all.

Faith that drives out demons

The mission entrusted by Christ to his Church entails the driving out of demons, that is, evil spirits. There are many idols, ideologies, and evil spirits besetting today's humanity. They damage many people's lives and infect our society and culture. It is through authentic faith that believers unmask all these demons and so gradually drive them out. Demons that immediately come to mind are idols like violence, consumerism, growth mania, money mania, the undermining of the opposition in one's own country and Church, and particularly the mutual subversion in international relations with its threats of mutual destruction. All this takes on demonic dimensions, against which diplomacy and psychology — important though they be — are powerless. We need faith, reliance on the power of God.

In a world where God is denied or his name is taboo, the devil and his work prosper unusually well. While in Russia, I was surprised to hear how frequently people, raised in atheism, use such expressions as "to the devil with you!" In a pagan world where Christ is still unknown, but also in a traditionalist context where many precepts and doctrines are known but the Christ of the Gospel is only superficially known, there exists a strange mixture of superstition and fear of evil spirits.

Among many tribes and in some ancestral cultures around the globe there is still a widespread fear of witches and all kinds of witchcraft. Whenever serious affliction comes to such people by way of sickness, sterility, miscarriage, the death of a loved one, or other calamities, they tremble in fear of evil spirits, and look for "evil" men or women who might be agents of the evil spirits (witches) acting out of jealousy, enmity, or in a vindictive spirit. This greatly aggravates the anguish, destroys relationships, and creates a pernicious atmosphere of suspicion leading to various types of persecution. Innocent people are suspected, persecuted, and tortured, forced into false confessions in a world poisoned by cruelty. This is surely an atmosphere in which the "princes of darkness" can use their weaponry of deception and hatred.

In reaction to the above there has developed in many regions an anti-magic mechanism, a system of divination to detect witches, rules of rituals and sacrifices, with all their diabolical divinations. When we read about these practices in African, Asian, or other non-Christian countries, we should not forget that similar perversities exist within Christian groups. A certain kind of ritualism and exorcism has become a form of anti-magic "medicine," even for some Catholics: a strange "therapy" somehow caught in a vortex of collective insanity. How can we meet this genuine cry for help from superstitious and really tormented people, who tolerate such practices by magic/anti-magic priests?

I hope the reader will bear with me if I respond by giving my personal experience in Bavaria, where I taught moral theology over thirty years ago. Many rural people came to our monastery when calamities happened on their farms — trouble with livestock and such. They just asked to have objects blessed as a kind of immunization. I was frequently called to dispense these blessings, and gradually I developed my own "ritual" when I saw that the people suspected certain persons as being the cause of the calamity. By blessing their objects it would appear that I was approving their suspicions, but I did not refuse to give the blessings. I would do it, however, only after a serious discussion in which I explained that the evil spirits could not enter their barn, their stall, or their chamber unless they had opened doors and windows for them. The main doors were suspicion, enmity, bitterness, and failure to forgive their neighbors' wrongs. The open windows were greed and similar vices. My blessing would help only if they were converted and closed their minds, their hearts, and their homes to such evil spirits.

Usually, the people would then make a good confession and go home with renewed heart and the blessed objects. When they felt blest they sent others to me telling them, however, about my "procedure." What I tried to do was to awaken healing faith and trust in God and renewed love of neighbor — a kind of logotherapy — without refusing the highly esteemed symbols of God's blessing. I am convinced that the liberating, healing Church should not neglect the use of symbols which stimulate healed memories.

Faith healing

Faith healing has risen to prominence in the Anglo-American context of revival movements. The modern charismatic renewal has helped to make it more attractive. It correctly emphasizes the function of faith in healing relationships.

It is impossible to find a common denominator for the manifold phenomena exhibited by the various kinds of faith healing, especially if we include the influential and fast-growing "healing churches" of Africa. So much is time-bound and culturally conditioned. Usually, there is a sound kernel of truth that is revealed after peeling away sundry enthusiastic exaggerations.

Here are some of the prominent features that are found almost everywhere in this field: a high appreciation of prayer as an expression of trust in God, the role of the faith community, the call to great trust in God's love and power, praise of God for his healing love, the role of charismatic personalities within a community of believers. The unique cult of a charismatic healer or the ways in which the enthusiasm is expressed may sometimes seem strange. However, this should not keep us from recognizing the value of enthusiastic faith and trust in God, particularly when they lead to the praise of God and a sense of gratitude permeating all of life.

The Catholic charismatic renewal movement and the neo-pentecostalism within the Anglican, Lutheran, and Methodist churches, rightly places more emphasis on the faith community than on individual healers. The individual charisma is seen within the charisma of the healing community.

There is a dangerous tendency here to assure those who seek healing that they will be healed if they "have enough faith." But to assure a sick person with these words is an illegitimate appropriation of the unique prerogative of Jesus to himself. A harmful side effect is that the sick person, who, in fact, is not healed in spite of his or her faith, may feel guilty of not having enough faith or, at least, may feel judged so by others.

Here, too, we should exercise caution about certain tendencies of specific healing sects. These sects frequently focus on the miraculous, the extraordinary, which is then used to prove the truth of the sect and/or the miraculous power of their charismatic leaders. This, too, is the reason why they look mainly for instantaneous healing. Of course, this is not to deny that God can intervene in most extraordinary ways. Our emphasis, however, is not on the miraculous but on the ongoing healing, the gradual healing of persons and relationships, the great impact of the spiritual dimension on the total psychosomatic reality, and the prime importance of the faith community, personal faith and trust in God.

But at the same time we must agree with M. T. Kelsey in his *Healing and Christianity:* "Healing is always a miracle . . . and never more so than when its center is the greatest of all miracles — Love." Faith healing has its center in God who is Love. It helps people to discover in themselves the image of God. Loving believers awaken in others faith in Love and invite them lovingly to let the Spirit dwell in their hearts. The person who lets love work consciously in all his or her life is truly on the way to wholeness, integration, healing, and ever more conformation with Christ the Healer and the healing community, where all praise the miracles of God's love and where faith bears fruit in love.

As is evident from the foregoing pages, the first concern of this book is an all-embracing understanding of salvation and truly human health through a biblical blending of the therapeutic nature of the proclamation and the celebration of salvation. And while the charisma of each individual is highly esteemed, we wish to place more emphasis on the inner resources of all, awakened by the Spirit, and the healing of the faith community in a vital manifestation of the solidarity of salvation.

Last but not least, the Church gives and must give positive attention to transforming frustrating suffering — insofar as it is expression of a fallen, frustrated world and history — into a redeemed and redeeming suffering. It is the physician's duty to fight against unbearable pain, while it is the graced mission of the faithful and the faith community to discover the deep meaning of suffering in the light of redemption. This was the meaning that gave Saint Paul "happiness" in his "way of helping to complete, in my poor human flesh, the full tale of Christ's afflictions still to be endured" (Colossians 1:24). This discovery and acceptance is truly a way to wholeness, to healing and saving relationships, and provides added strength to bolster up our efforts for truly human health.

Liberating power of preparing for death

The apostle of the Gentiles crowns his praise of the redemption with his hymn on liberation "from the law of sin and death" (Romans 8:2). Those who are enslaved by psychic and social blocks and are constantly tormented by them cannot reconcile themselves with their own mortality, their prospect of death. They cannot face death with serenity. But we are all on the road to death, and by redemption are destined to reach in death the pinnacle of our fullness of being. Those whose purpose of life fails to recognize the positive meaning of death are not able to live an authentic life. They are unable to discover their unique calling and the One who calls them into being and into the fullness of life which is climaxed at death. Their whole existence is steeped in triviality; they remain lonely persons in a crowd of depersonalized people.

Those who, on the contrary, are reconciled with their mortality and are prepared to die their own death in final trust gain a rich measure of freedom to live an authentic life and to pursue their purpose in life unwaveringly.

The faith we celebrate and which graces us with salvation and wholeness, the faith which grants us true life, has its deepest roots in the death of Christ which, in combination with his Resurrection, is the source of our redemption. Because of our expectation of resurrection we can say "Yes" to death at the very moment it strikes.

Liberated in Christ from the prospect of a meaningless death, we acquire a new caring, a new solicitude for life but also for the death which is meant for us by God, our Creator and Redeemer. Death thus becomes our time of fulfillment, our day of harvest, our hour of homecoming.

This Christian solicitude for a mature death in final trust liberates us for our life here and now, day by day. In the light of death thus understood — with Christ as *kairos* (the great hour destined by God) — the believer discovers in each moment the challenge and unique offer of a fruitful life. Through reconciliation with one's mortality in the light of the Paschal mystery, the door is also open for a redeeming appreciation of suffering and illness, which in turn leads to true wholeness and authenticity.

Those who are prepared for death, understood as the final call and homecoming of the Lord, will never jeopardize their lives and health senselessly. The salvation message is a mighty warning against all kinds of unseemly, untimely dying: not only against suicide but also against accidental death caused by lack of responsibility, loss of health and early death through alcoholism and other addictions — including smoking and other unhealthy life-styles. Reverence for the presence of the Lord of life and death also obligates all to a more acute ecological consciousness.

Pastors, families, friends, and members of the healing and caring professions should make use of the many expressions of affirmation, loving care, and faith witness to assist the dying in their final "Yes." For this purpose, all should cultivate a basic knowledge of the psychology of the dying, the phases through which the sick normally come to their full acceptance and meaning of death. We must try to understand what the dying are trying to tell us in order to find the appropriate word and gesture in response.

Reconciled with Brother Death and prepared to die our own death, we can ever better understand what it means for human wholeness and health to be reconciled with God, with neighbor, and with ourselves. It is in these areas that the power of faith shines through.

Chapter Six

WOUNDED HEALERS IN A WOUNDED WORLD

Our divine Savior is himself the archetype of the "wounded healer." In Christ we see the fulfillment of what Second Isaiah foretold about the Servant of God:

> He was despised, he shrank from the sight of men,
>   tormented and humbled by suffering;
>   we despised him, we held him of no account,
>   a thing from which men turn away their eyes.
> Yet on himself he bore our sufferings,
>   our torments he endured . . .
>   and by his scourging we are healed (Isaiah 53:3-5).

Jesus, the divine and human Physician, is more deeply wounded than any other human being; and all his wounds and all his sufferings are intimately linked with his mission as our Savior and Healer. The mystery of this utter solidarity between the Healer and those to be healed should be seen as the key to authentic healing from the perspective of salvation.

Each Christian can share in his or her own way in the healing ministry of Christ. All are called to enter as completely as possible into the dimension of saving solidarity. But all of us, too, are wounded by our own sins and shortcomings; and the more consciously and humbly we accept this fact, the better we can heal and help.

In the following two chapters we will focus on the healing-caring professions of today's society and, then, on Church ministry and the Church community as a whole.

Healer and patient at the same time, all of us are partially contaminated by the various sicknesses in our environment and wounded by the solidarity of sin. Yet, we all receive redeeming and healing powers from a saving solidarity in Christ, and the more we dedicate ourselves to our redemptive and healing mission the more we can be freed from sin-solidarity.

We discuss here, first of all, the members of the healing profession because not only are they faced constantly with suffering but the very suffering of those for whom they lovingly care touches them deeply, burdens them, and can wound them. This is particularly true in cases where psychotherapists enter into a very demanding relationship with their patients. On the occasion of a "transfer" they experience, painfully, their own wounds and their vulnerability. The sometimes troublesome reactions of a patient can wound them, especially because of their deep compassion and dedication. Carl Gustav Jung developed the archetype of the "wounded healer" from his own experiences. The archetype indicates symbolically a profound "knowledge about a wound by which the healer suffers with his patient."

Jung emphasizes one of the therapist's risks. The patients' emotions can have a contaminating effect: they find a kind of resonance in the therapist's nervous system, especially during psychoanalysis. As a consequence, psychotherapists and other therapists can become somehow unsettled. This is one of the factors of the transfer whenever there are deep feelings of solidarity between therapist and patient.

This has much to do with Christ, who compassionately bears our burden in order to save us. Healing love strengthens the identity and integrity of the healer or helper, but because of the healer's own wounds various tensions can arise. Wounds not yet fully healed may once more become painful.

Dignity and risks of the healing professions

In all religions and cultures the healing professions are held in high regard and enjoy social prestige; and as a group they have tried to remain worthy of these honors by upholding and maintaining a high level of ethical standards.

The healing-helping professions (physicians, psychotherapists, nurses, social workers, child-care personnel, etc.) need a considerable degree of altruism, sensitivity, and trustworthiness. To the extent that they fulfill their task responsibly and with competence, they participate in the redeeming, healing ministry of Christ. But it must be emphasized that, according to the biblical message of redemption, the indispensable call to conversion and renewal includes the healers and helpers as well as the patients and those who need help. Also, the institutions dedicated to healing are in constant need of renewal. All who proclaim salvation and intend to be servants of reconciliation, liberation, and healing are in need of the Divine Healer and of mutual support.

Those young men and women who throughout the ages entered into religious communities dedicated to the care of the sick and aged, and generously served the most desperate needs with very restricted means, knew that such a profession requires a great and steadfast idealism. It means nothing less than a vocation to "be-for-others," to bear the burden of others. For Christians, this means to point, with all one's life, to Christ who came to bear our burdens, the divine-human Physician "through whose wounds we are healed."

The healing professions have much in common with the priestly vocation. In fact, in some cultures these two vocations often were not distinct from each other: they were presumed to be closely related because of their pronounced mutuality of vision and endeavor. Both healers and priests tried to interpret life's deeper meaning: existence in troublesome situations.

Through the centuries, however, the healing and priestly professions had their difficulties. There arose, time and again, conflicts, misunderstandings, and jealousies between healers and priests. Even professional groups striving for high ideals and noble ethical standards are tempted by sin, by unknown powers of the subconscious and of collective egotism. They were living proof that everyone is in need of redemption and purification.

Within Christianity, which focuses on the blending of love of God and love of neighbor — especially the needy neighbor — the healing, caring, helping professions are highly relevant. Without them, a full testimony to salvation and complete proclamation of the Good News are hardly thinkable. But this does not imply that these professions have a monopoly on altruism, so much so that others are not called to heal, to care, and to help. Those others, however, should keep in healthy contact with these particular professions in order to share in their knowledge and technique.

In his apostolic letter *Salvifici Doloris* (#29), Pope John Paul II pays tribute to all the men and women throughout the world who are dedicated to healing and helping, to overcoming hatred, violence, cruelty, contempt for persons, and insensitivity or indifference to sufferers. He stresses the fact that the Church sees them all as workers in solidarity with Christ, the merciful Samaritan. They live an essential dimension of the Gospel by actively refusing to remain passive when faced with suffering. They will certainly hear the words of Jesus on Judgment Day: "Anything you did for one of my brothers here, however humble, you did for me" (Matthew 25:40). The Day of Resurrection will reveal both the redeeming power of suffering in conformity with Christ and the healing love for those who suffer.

All this should make clear how much the members of the healing, helping, caring professions deserve our grateful love, our support, and a more appreciative interpretation of their mission through the pastoral ministry of the Church. Those healers or helpers who, in the process of altruistic dedication, have suffered specifically deserve sensitive and therapeutic help from the whole community and, especially, from qualified therapists and priests. Healers who have truly found refuge in a faith community are better able to withstand the risks ordinarily taken by vulnerable and wounded healers than others who lack such support.

If it is true that physicians and other members of the healing professions often neither seek nor accept timely help for themselves — as certain writers claim — it is even more tragic when there is lack of pastoral sensitivity and assistance for these dedicated men and women, who spend their best lives in the service of others. A practical question, however, is whether many theologians and pastors are aware of this problem and are capable of fulfilling their role in union and cooperation with members of the healing profession.

"Helpless Helpers"

After so much empirical research, it is no longer possible to doubt the fact that in countries where the model of "health industry" is most developed, members of the healing professions, working within this system, are often more plagued by depressions and suicidal tendencies than the ordinary citizen. This is a definite challenge not only to the existing modern technical model and the various institutions of "health delivery" but also to theologians and to priests who are in actual pastoral care.

In his book dealing with "Helpless Helpers," which has gained much attention but also some sharp criticism, the psychotherapist Wolfgang Schmidbauer points to the "helper's syndrome" as the main cause of these cases of depression among men and women of the helping and healing professions. He looks for causes in experiences during early childhood which might have triggered the choice of these professions and a somehow unhealthy approach to them. In the tenth edition, after many discussions with representatives of social sciences, he shows that he is willing to take more carefully into account the social-environmental causes of "helper's syndrome." He now agrees with many of those in the healing profession that the present model should be revised.

Schmidbauer's intention is not to belittle the evident altruism within these professions and among those persons who suffer from the "helper's syndrome." On the contrary, he is convinced that the syndrome, in its mild forms, can even reinforce the altruism. The goal of healing is to provide for a more healthy, more creative, and more helpful expression of genuine altruism.

The more serious forms of "helper's syndrome" refer to the wounding experiences of the unwanted child or the child subjected to authoritarian parents and educators. Driven by an unrealistic idealism, such a helper or healer can be obsessed by the thought — in itself right — that those entrusted to "my care" should not suffer "as I did" from a lack of attention and affirmation. However, the overpowering superego (heritage of the authoritarian figure) and the suffering from the inability to live consistently on the level of his or her high ideal can lead to inflexibility toward self and toward those under his or her care.

These mostly unconscious forces make impossible a healthy exchange between persons. There is, instead, a one-way relationship. Under the pressure of this syndrome, the helpers want to give but do not allow themselves consciously to want a return in the form of gratitude, affection, or affirmation. They do not seek from the cared-for person the creative and rewarding contribution of co-responsibility, for they are unable to acknowledge to themselves or to their patients that they, too, are wounded and constantly in need of mutual support. Their refusal to consciously recognize their hunger and thirst for mutuality — which is even more impatient at the unconscious and subconscious level — blocks the way to healthy and healing relationships.

The "helper's syndrome" also addicts one to a total dedication to the healing-helping profession while neglecting the private sphere — the needs of one's family, oneself, and others, which make themselves known but are not recognized. Thus, the "wounded healer" cannot operate effectively in his or her personal life.

The above-mentioned Schmidbauer, a psychoanalyst and therapist, asserts that this danger exists particularly among psychoanalysts and the various schools of psychotherapy, where he has discovered much intolerance, jealousy, and distrust. This kind of distrust is reflected, unavoidably, in the relationship between individual therapists.

Helpers affected by this syndrome feel at home with sick people or others entrusted to them if, because of "regressive neuroses," these people like to be "mothered" and tutored. And if a patient refuses this kind of relationship, they complain about lack of gratitude, while otherwise they like to assure themselves and others that they do not at all depend on thankfulness. Another doctor-therapist, J. Willi, writes that "it can be observed that nurses find more satisfaction in caring for a totally helpless patient than for one who gradually regains his or her autonomy."

The "helper's syndrome" can become epidemic in psychiatric institutions. Psychiatrists have to look for order and discipline; and as a result they are tempted to look only for submissiveness in patients instead of encouraging responsibility and constructive cooperation.

It is no wonder that this syndrome played a noticeable role within the Church, whose moral and pastoral theology and practice centered on obedience and docility. It also produced authoritarian churchmen, preconditioned for it by their own upbringing. Church leaders and all the healing and social professions should concentrate more on education for freedom: encouragement of growth in responsible, creative freedom. The more our healers, helpers, pastoral workers accept, freely and consciously, their own wounds and scars, the less will be their danger of falling into the "helper's syndrome." At least its grave forms can be more easily avoided in this way.

A healthy sense of thankfulness, a consciousness that we all are in need of affirmation and acceptance, and a gracious kind of helpfulness for others — all this has a healing power and promotes healthy relationships everywhere. But an imagined selflessness that makes one feel, "I can serve the others, but I don't need them," hinders one from reaching a healthy understanding and realization of the commandment, "Love thy neighbor as thyself."

The psychiatrist Stanley A. Leavy feels that a main cause of the susceptibility of many physicians and psychotherapists to this damaging syndrome is their aloofness about the idea of transcendence. Among others, he mentions Sigmund Freud, who followed a widespread trend that denied any authentic experience of a transcendent reality. Describing any faith in a personal God as unhealthy and neurotic, he felt obliged to interpret human existence and human health without — and even in opposition to — religion.

No wonder, then, that some famous and not-so-famous representatives of the healing profession think they can act at playing God. In this way they deprive their patients of co-responsibility, making them believe they have no freedom. Both Leavy and Karl Menninger speak of atheistic psychoanalysts who boast that, by their treatment, they "freed" their patients from religious belief. Actually, this is the result of manipulation and/or of a counter-transference, done frequently with strong arguments for unbelief. When this type of procedure is merged with a philosophy and psychology of self-centered "self-fulfillment," we are faced with a dangerous contamination of patients by doctors who transmit one of the most devastating illnesses of our time.

In the same context Leavy warns representatives of religion that they can seriously damage the psychic health of believers if they do not allow them any kind of doubt about religious matters or about a doctor's own principles, thus blocking the inborn desire for sincere search for more light. Those who, in the name of human authority or even worse in the name of religion, try to impose on persons under their care a whole package of doctrines and laws without allowing the patient any personal insights are surely not healers. Such people are sick; they are contaminated authority figures who can be healed only when they humbly acknowledge their wounds, their ills, and their insensitivity.

Senior citizens as wounded healers

In all its manifold expressions, cheerful caring is a privileged dimension of the healing mission. It prevents many psychic wounds, cures others, and has many positive psychosomatic values. It is particularly beneficial in caring for the aged.

Care for our senior citizens presents a serious social problem in our urban industrial society with its high proportion of nuclear families. Retirement, being cut off suddenly from their everyday working environment and habits while still in good physical and psychic health, finds many people unprepared to use and enjoy leisure time. They feel lost, empty. There can be a painful feeling of being no longer of use to anyone, a feeling of isolation and loneliness. Others, relegated to nursing homes, feel exiled from their former homes, neglected by their relatives and old friends. There is also the gradual experience of more and more discomfort from failing sight, hearing, and mobility as they reach the final stages of life. All this cries to the Church, as well as to society, for healing and caring, for the good Samaritan.

And now the Church is discovering that the senior citizens themselves can be an almost inexhaustible reservoir of Samaritans, wounded healers who, like the *elders* of the earliest Christian tradition, are willing and able to bring their life experience and their generosity creatively into the life of the community. This is true for both women and men. The decrease in traditional priestly vocations is a challenge to the Church to rediscover the rich potential of gifted "elders." A high percentage of those who now retire around their sixtieth year could and should be prepared to share in the mission of the Church, to proclaim the Good News, to heal and to care.

Both Church and society have to revise their ideas about the elderly. One idea is to offer them ample opportunity for ongoing education. Our society is in error if it neglects this because it might lack market value. This very attitude is one of the destructive illnesses of our society: that it measures values by market standards while overlooking so many things of higher value.

Ongoing education could be an interdisciplinary endeavor to communicate and deepen our own insights on aging, the role of the elderly, their problems and potentialities. We would find that persons of this age group not only can better recognize their own situation but also can help others to resolve their problems in a creative way and put their capacities to the service of those aging persons who are most in need.

The Church should offer some preparatory training to senior citizens who are willing to volunteer to help in the pastoral care of the aged and lonely. In accord with the Letter of Saint James (5:14), "elders" can pray for and with the sick and suffering, bless them, allow them to talk trustfully of their past failings, and bring to them the joy of faith. The question of whether these elders of today could be ordained for administering the Anointing of the Sick could easily be resolved; but, in any case, they would be the ones best able to prepare their contemporaries for the consolation of the sacraments.

Activation of our senior citizens would mean that many aging persons could be spared isolation in poorly run nursing homes. In various parts of the world, senior citizens have already organized regular visits to the lonely — visits whose purpose is to console, to cheer, to help, and to bring the good news of healing love.

A modern revival of the ancient institute of the "elders" and "widows" could bring new contributing forces to the whole pastoral and healing mission of the Church. And, in this, many people could find, in the last decades of their life, their highest fulfillment by becoming helpers of the Divine Healer.

Family as wounded healers

The social and humane sciences have studied the manifold interactions of individual, family, cultural, and socioeconomic life. The interactions within the family and of the family within its total environment powerfully affect each other. The good and healthy elements as well as the vulnerability and wounds of the individual family members affect the family, while the family as a whole has its particular influence on the world around it. The environment can be a great threat and danger, especially for those families who have not realized their shared responsibilities.

In a Christian vision, the family is called to be a salvific community dedicated to the wholeness, integrity, and salvation of each member. And the family as a whole can be for many people a "sacrament," as it were, through its example of healing solidarity. But it also is vulnerable in the area of mutual exchange among its members and those same members with the world community. The more the family dedicates itself to healing wounds and reconciling people, the more it can — as a "wounded healer" — deal with the pernicious forces in and around itself.

The greatest healing power of the family is the mutual love of its members, which means mutual affirmation, faithfulness, and readiness to forgive and to be reconciled. This is logotherapy at its best.

The social professions and their respective institutions are mostly busy repairing hurts and wounds which arise within the families or afflict them through an unhealthy world around them. This fact poses the question to Church and society: Are we doing enough to keep families healthy and to sensitize them to their responsibility to become healthy and healing powers for their environment, their society, and their state? Are we doing enough to create good economic, social, and cultural conditions for them? Is enough done to prepare the young generation for marriage and family life?

If all members of the social service and healing professions receive the necessary formation and support, they can do much to assist and to heal sick and endangered families, and thereby can learn much that will contribute creatively to their own families. But as we have seen in our reflections on the "helper's syndrome," it is possible for them to become so busy in their service for others that they gravely neglect their own families and most intimate relationships.

If a professional career, even of the healing and helping professions, is given *absolute* priority, damage will be felt on all sides.

But it is not a truly healing or helping activity if it becomes a flight from one's own problems and from the family. Typical might be the statement of a doctor: ''Since my wife can find no acceptable solution for fertility control, she refuses to sleep with me. I am hurt, but I don't tell her. So I feel much more at ease in the clinic and go home late.'' The wife complains that her husband has no time for her. She feels jealous of her husband's patients and becomes increasingly critical, which drives the husband still further into his professional overactivity.

Even worse is the situation when one partner is so much the slave of a success-oriented culture that he lets himself become totally absorbed in his drive for more and more money, which is his only idea of ''success.'' This is one of the reasons for the malady inflicting Western culture, which seems obsessed with a quantitive growth mania encouraged by manipulative advertising that lures families into ever-increasing consumption and continues to intrude more and more on family life. Spouses have no time for each other; parents have no time for their children, so they give them an abundance of material things but not themselves. Add to all this a prevailing individualistic world view which induces everyone to think in terms of his or her own ''self-fulfillment.'' This, too, can become an addiction and a cause of other addictions.

Strained relationships cause many kinds of psychosomatic disorders and can destroy one's spiritual well-being. A family exposed to these risks must begin to understand itself as a healing community, and each member must see his or her role as ''wounded healer.'' If this is done, usually these dangers can be avoided.

Happy family life is based on an unchanging mutual dependence. Each person possesses positive, healing powers, but also some negative, harmful failings. Those who enter marriage dreaming about an idyll of life with an absolutely ideal partner will sooner or later be rudely awakened. The task for each partner is to love the other as he or she really is, to accept the other in his or her composite reality. This will more easily succeed if each spouse sees himself or herself as "wounded" and, therefore, in need of a healer, but at the same time as "healer" with powerful inner strengths for both self-healing and for encouraging the other to discover his or her similar resources. This means that both husband and wife must view each other as healer for the "wounded healer."

The opposite choice is the useless and frustrating play of the game called "if only," "yes, but." (Dr. Berne, in his *Games People Play,* cites this as one of the games that people play.) These poor players are victims of feelings of helplessness, impotent yearnings, a desire to be cared for, "mothered," while at the same time they make affirmation by the partner almost impossible. Therapy is not easy, but these people are direly in need of help. A first step is to help them to understand how noxious is the game they are playing. What has been said in the previous chapter about the healing power of the biblical virtues can be helpful therapy here.

Alcoholics Anonymous as wounded healers

A fitting example of the "wounded healer" in today's society can be seen in the members of Alcoholics Anonymous. They have the courage to tell their story, to show their wounds, and to acknowledge their failures. Each one lets the group know that "I am not any better than you," and each one tells the story of how he or she found strength through help from other anonymous alcoholics. All share the profound conviction that "If I, with all my scars, could do it, surely you can too!"

This model is no longer restricted to the healing of alcoholics; its powerful dynamics are now being used in other areas as well. One example is the excellent book *On Becoming a New Person,* by

Philip St. Romain. My own experience of being completely larynxectomized gives me a unique opportunity to help others who are or will soon be in the same situation. Especially those who, like myself, experience setbacks should be encouraged not to give up, but to muster their inner strengths to search for more profound values to aid in readjustment. It is well known that the best helpers of cancer patients can be others who have experienced the same problems and are still faced with them. It is to be hoped that doctors and the Church will learn to mobilize these wounded healers.

Wounded healers and the civic community

Healing of the civic community is one of the great themes and dimensions of social ethics. The major part of Volume III of my work *Free and Faithful in Christ* is dedicated to this theme. Here, I will treat only some aspects of the topic. We all suffer somehow from the evils, disorders, and dangerous, contagious trends of our surroundings, our socioeconomic society and culture. None of us is free from all the pitfalls. Our criticism will be constructive in this area only if our proposals and our endeavors recognize both aspects of the situation: that we can and must work for the healing of at least some facets of the civic community and that we acknowledge that we, too, are affected by the virus, that we ourselves are wounded and are actually a part of the problem.

If we really commit ourselves to some effort for a healthier civic community, we must not only talk — yes, dialogue is important here — but we must also take action. For instance, as soon as it was determined that cigarette smoking is the most important single factor in developing lung cancer, many doctors stopped smoking almost immediately. They felt that, as doctors, they would lose credibility in their own eyes as well as in their patients' eyes if they continued as if they were not conscious of the dangers. If a doctor is not willing or not able to stop, he will not have the courage, generally speaking, to tell a patient frankly, "Your disease is your heavy smoking." Rather, he will prefer to ignore the situation.

If we commit ourselves, together with others, to the healing of the civic community in some of the most urgent aspects of our sick culture — consumerism, corrupt politics, and so on — we will gradually discover our own share, our own complicity in the sickness, although heretofore it might have been hidden from our sight.

Members of the healing and helping professions need and often leave room for gratuitous services above and beyond what is required in a culture which values only what can be sold. Their dedication to the sick and needy where they can get no remuneration or satisfaction is of great value in healing one dimension of our culture. Wolfgang Schmidbauer, whom I have quoted on his research on the "helper's syndrome," is very conscious of the genuine altruism in these professions. "The modern industrial society is beginning to suffer so much under the constraints of quantitative growth and 'progress' that it is forced to allow cavities where its value-system is waived. And I think that real changes will happen in and around these cavities."

For these reasons and many others, it is regrettable that vocations for healing and helping professions in religious life are decreasing. Religious Orders should be acutely aware that they also have a mission for healing the civic community. Their members, almost unavoidably, are "wounded" to some extent, contaminated by the sickness of the culture. But becoming fully conscious of this and trusting in the healing power of Christ through faith, they can become more effective healers, while never denying to either themselves or others that they are, just like others, "wounded healers."

Chapter Seven

THE CHURCH: A WOUNDED HEALER

The main concern of our reflections in this book has been the Church's total mission to proclaim the gospel of salvation and peace and to heal. We mean the Church in all her dimensions: the People of God, the teaching and learning Church, the pilgrim Church, the celebrating Church, and every facet of the proclaiming and healing Church — all, of course, from the aspect of "wounded healer."

Healing power of wounded priests

All the faithful together make up the "priestly people of God"; all are called and enabled to "adore God in spirit and truth." Such adoration has in itself the most potent healing energies. Here, however, we speak of the ministerial priesthood, including the pope, the bishops, priests, and deacons, whose most noble and pressing task is to strive as pastors, together with all the faithful, to become ever more truly adorers "in spirit and truth," thus to be light of the world and salt to the earth.

In common with the healing professions, priests have many opportunities to heal; but they also have many risks, as we saw in the previous chapter. The more they are as conscious of being wounded and vulnerable as of being gifted with healing powers, the more the Savior and Divine Healer will make them partners in his mission to proclaim the saving news and to heal.

As a member of a theological community, my thoughts first turn to "the wounded theologian." Theologians have to be men or women filled with compassion, ready to suffer and to be misunderstood in the fulfillment of a prophetic role, sharply aware of their vulnerability. They must be alert to the danger of allowing themselves to be contaminated by a vague spirit of the era, by harmful trends of the culture, and by a desire for being left in peace and quiet when they should be making bold to meet Jesus on the stormy sea.

Theologians must be especially aware that they and their theology are sick if they lack pastoral-mindedness, the dynamic to heal and to reconcile, to expose the true character of false ideologies, and to reveal the true image of God. Theologians, and those who follow their teachings, can be dangerously contaminated by a spirit of triumph within a success-oriented culture and educational system or by a code of law and mere obedience combined with an unchecked authoritarian-type superego: bowing before those who can remunerate or promote, while scorning those who have nothing to offer.

We recall the proud titles, honors, and careers inherited from the era of feudalism, bringing with them the many dangers that lead to

113

improper motivation. Just as bishops, in spite of all their good will, can become captives in elaborate but uninhabitable palaces, so professors and famous theologians can dwell aloof in their ego-built "palaces" of fame and honors.

We know of theologians who were or are sincere searchers for truth, zealous for people's salvation, dedicated to a therapeutic theology, but who felt threatened by this kind of theology when they were treated badly by authorities who misunderstood them. Their deep wounds have made them become timid or even bitter, sometimes to the point of being unable to heal others.

We see before us a great company of zealous priests who are wearing themselves out physically, psychically, spiritually, in continuous activity for their flock. The syndrome of activity increases under the pressure of a society in which quantitative achievement is especially honored. Then, there is that great number of unsatisfied, frustrated priests who, by their example, discourage priestly vocations.

Many are wounded so deeply because they do not grasp the true identity of their vocation and are unable to discern the signs of the times. Some have received a lopsided formation marked by legalism in moral theology, formalism in liturgy, and a static view of the Church. How can they feel at home in a Church which, according to the Second Vatican Council, understands herself as a pilgrim Church? There are also priests who gladly accept the Pastoral Constitution on the Church but are unable (and are not helped) to find for themselves an interpretation of ministerial priesthood corresponding to it. In their confusion, many find it difficult to accept the co-responsibility and cooperation of lay people.

In all of us there is still a hidden "atheist" who wounds and threatens us. Here I call to mind, especially, the kind of atheism which has found its classical expression in Ernst Bloch. He denies the existence of a personal God, Creator, and Redeemer because he refuses to be a recipient of gifts that oblige him to be grateful. Activists, who not only neglect the spiritual-contemplative dimension of faith but also trust more in their work than in God's grace, stress their own achievements and require remuneration for everything in one form or another. In reality, their attitude is like that of Bloch and his kind of atheism; but they do not try to play God in the way he does.

Priests of all ranks who are addicted to activism can suffer severe forms of the "helper's syndrome." Spending their energy and time for others, they want no one to contradict them, no one to refuse the kind of dependence they want to impose. They don't realize that, just as much as those entrusted to them, they need to be grateful recipients; they need affirmation, encouragement, and correction in order to remain whole and healthy.

Under the impact of certain structures and expectations many priests, especially those in the higher ranks, do not come to a balanced blend and healthy distinction between their office and their person. They play "your excellency" even in their personal relationships.

All these wounds can be aggravated by a harmful "transfer," especially in the case of people with regressive neuroses who seek security and escape from personal responsibility in total surrender to the priest. This happens particularly if the priest is strongly ruled by his superego and an authoritarian understanding of his role. Since he is not aware of being wounded, both persons become more feeble, less capable of healthy and healing relationships.

Another kind of wound is marked by a wavering between ambition and resignation. The more intense the ambition — fed by the environment and by an established system of promotion and "persona" cult — the more vehement the reaction of resignation and depression.

What we priests all need is to have the courage to face our vulnerability and our being wounded in various ways, to put our trust in the Divine Healer and to join him humbly in the dual mission of messengers of salvation and ministers of healing. This demands of us an acute awareness of mutual dependence and a reverential readiness to receive as well as to give in all our dealings.

Wounded Church in a wounded culture

Faced as we are with the problems of the institutional and structural dimensions of the Church in interaction with society and culture, we must not seek escape by slipping into a disembodied image of the Church. We love the real Church in spite of her imperfect institutions, practices, laws, and appurtenances. But we must not forget that in all her dimensions, even those of administration and organization, the Church is called to be and should become ever more a ''sacrament of salvation and healing.'' All her life in all its facets should point to Christ, the Savior and Healer. This will not happen automatically. If there is not an ongoing renewal and healing, some institutional elements can even become countersigns rather than signs.

The Second Vatican Council meditated deeply on the mutual relationships and interactions between Church and world, receiving and giving (The Church Today, #40-44), and on the complex relation between the proclamation of salvation and culture (Church's Missionary Activity, #58,62, and throughout).

Because of her generous endeavor to bring an ever-new enculturation of her message, institutional forms, theological and liturgical language (including symbols and signs), and philosophy into all living cultures of the inhabited earth, the Church acquires abundant cultural wealth. Enculturation, together with ongoing dialogue, counteracts the dangers of enshrining the mystery of faith in one set of formulations, resulting in a loss of contact with people's lives and — this is the most dangerous malady — forgetting that the mystery of salvation is always infinitely greater than any human language. The very effort to create uniformity of doctrine through a single dead language destroys the vitality of the salvation message and its healing-saving power within the dynamics of salvation history.

Local churches, which attempt enculturation but do not remain in contact and dialogue with the center of the Church and with other local churches of other cultures, will easily be contaminated by cultural narrowness. After a time they are unable to distinguish adequately abiding truth from time-bound expressions. A centralistic Church government was not better off when it lived in alliance with and strict dependence on just one culture or one language group.

The great schisms from the eleventh to the sixteenth century and the splitting of the Protestant Church into numerous separate denominations were largely due to cultural, social, and political causes. The less conscious were the churchmen of the destructive union within a narrow political and cultural system, the more devastating was the impact of differing cultural and political interests in perpetuating alienation and enmity. What in reality is a fossilization of past adaptations (some authentic and some less acceptable) becomes sacralized, a cause of apathy and rejection. Therefore, John XXIII rightly urged the Second Vatican Council to make every effort to painstakingly discern between the abiding essence of revealed truth and its various time-bound and culturally conditioned expressions — a task which is anything but easy. (This the Council attempted in The Church Today, #62.)

In her relations with cultures, economic systems, philosophies, and styles of authority, the Church must be constantly aware that all this belongs to a world in need of redemption and actually redeemed only insofar as it is open to Christ, the Savior, Healer, and Servant. Moreover, the Church herself in her members, her structures, her use of philosophies and ideologies, while proclaiming the salvation message, can be more or less wounded and contaminated by the world around her and by the very historical-cultural means she uses to accomplish her mission. This contamination becomes acute where "sacred alliances between throne and altar" try to perpetuate past systems and privileges and where openness to the signs of the times is lacking.

Each adaptation is imperfect and necessarily calls for self-critique when new historical dimensions indicate the necessity of a fresh approach. Well-known examples of this are the following: a patriarchal family and social structure that is accepted without critical analysis and authoritarian monarchies and/or oligarchies. (Churchmen of the past, for example, used to speak of papal and episcopal "monarchy.")

When, partially under the very impact of the dynamics of revealed truth, new horizons develop, fresh symptoms of a "wounded Church" are bound to appear. These include uncritical new adaptations and an equally uncritical clinging to a fossilized past or imperfect enculturations. This polarization becomes worse when ideological justifications are made in the name of revelation.

The transition from a patriarchal family and an authoritarian society to partnership family and democracy is not easy. In the process of discerning the "signs of the times" painful tensions and polarizations arise. On the one hand, there are those wounded by an anti-authoritarian "spirit of the era"; and on the other hand, there are those who felt satisfied with an authoritarian education, a male-centered Church regimentation, to the point where they feel shocked by even small changes, such as the appearance of "altar girls" along with altar boys. Another example is the painful polarization between those who approve the arms race "for the defense of our culture" and those who, with great conviction, propose nonviolent defense as the only alternative for survival with dignity.

We all need deep faith and humility, trust in God, and sharp awareness of our own woundedness in order to fulfill our vocation to heal and to reconciliate within today's Church and society.

Since the Second Vatican Council the Church has grown in awareness of her wounds and of the need for healing and renewal. The World Council of Churches also calls attention to our wounded, divided Christianity in a lacerated world. Healing is urgent and possible if we put our trust in our Savior. If the various incrustations and cultural constraints are recognized for what they are, wounds can be healed more easily; the ecumenical dialogue can become more humble and promising. For all parts of Christianity it will be easier to withstand the temptation to absolutize man-made traditions which block the road to unity.

The sixth plenary assembly of the World Council of Churches in Vancouver, 1983, strongly emphasized "healing and reconciliation." There was a special commission on "sharing and healing." Painfully, these representatives of numerous segments of Christianity made note of "the fact that the churches have not yet sufficiently advanced in being a fellowship of confessing, of learning, of participation, of sharing, of healing, and of reconciliation, to overcome the stumbling blocks which have deeply divided them."

This is the sorry situation of a wounded healer. But it is much less deplorable than the attitude of past centuries, since now the churches recognize and humbly confess their shortcomings and wounds and are seeking healing in a new effort to attain mutual dependence. Obviously, there are better chances to gain attention and trust from a badly wounded world when Christian churches speak humbly and without self-righteousness, as "wounded healers" who draw our attention to the divine Savior.

Healing through service

As we saw earlier in this book, the proclamation of the kingdom of God through Jesus is inseparable from his new authority as the Servant of God and men. Hence, sharing in Christ's healing mission is unthinkable without joining Christ in his authority as the Servant. We learn to heal through service.

In his book *The Five Wounds of the Holy Church* (written in 1832), Rosmini, one of the greatest Catholic thinkers and reformers of his time, points expressly at the wounded Church government. He examines the "wound of the left hand" of the crucified Church and identifies it as the alienation of the clergy, their separateness from the people, manifesting itself singularly in the public cult (liturgy). He sees the "wound of the right hand" as the inadequate formation of the clergy, which alienates the priests from the rest of the faithful. The "wound of the heart" is the lack of unity and collegiality among priests and bishops, and the "wound of the left foot" is the alienated and noncollegial appointment of bishops.

Rosmini considers the cooperation of the clergy and the faithful in the election of their bishop "a divine right," explicitly acknowledging, however, that the modality must be determined according to the needs and possibilities of time and place. With astonishing frankness he deplores the centralistic appointment of local bishops, with total elimination of cooperation from the local clergy and the faithful. In his eyes this centralism was often accountable for simonistic maneuvers, but his emphasis is on his battle against the appointment of bishops through emperors, kings, and princes — rulers of people.

This was the main reason why the Hapsburg party considered Rosmini a most dangerous man. It did everything to discredit him, and managed to have his book put on the index of forbidden books.

The "wound of the right foot" is caused by assaults on the freedom of the Church. Rosmini suggests that the most effective way to remedy this is for the Church to free herself from earthly powers, from compromising alliances between throne and altar, and frankness within the Church. To ensure the Church's inner freedom he considers evangelical poverty as the most urgent remedy, in view of the Church's earthly possessions and their deviation from their original purpose. Repeatedly, he insists that the Church does not need treasures and privileges but, rather, the freedom to live her own life and to fulfill her mission faithfully, trusting in her Savior. Regarding the spirit of poverty, Rosmini holds that regular public accounting of the Church's holdings, its income and expenditures, is an indispensable remedy for her own healing and credibility: "How well would the church win the hearts of the faithful by doing so!" (The latest monetary scandals in the Church have proved how right he was.)

It would be a huge mistake to dismiss Rosmini with the words: "Physician, heal thyself." He was utterly sincere in his effort to make the Church aware of her wounds and her need for healing, so that she would become better able to perform both her role as messenger of salvation and minister of healing. In this way the Church would enjoy an ever-increasing wholeness and holiness. He directs our attention to Jesus, the divine-human Healer and Savior, and urges us to allow Jesus to heal us so that we can become more effectively "salt to the earth."

Rosmini serves notice to "yes-sayers" and flatterers who tell churchmen that everything is all right and whatever they do is excellent. His warning is even more severe for those who surround themselves with yes-sayers who "cover up wounds with what can only be called 'diplomatic hypocrisy.' "

From Rosmini we can learn a great lesson for our times: a combination of frankness and humility, readiness to suffer with the Church and for her, a great love of the Church and her leaders, and a burning desire that the Church may faithfully fulfill her healing ministry as a humble servant who is a "wounded healer."

Healing through a healthy life-style

The authority-service style which Rosmini so frankly and eloquently recommends for healing the five wounds of the Church is part of a broader concept of a healthy and healing life-style. We speak here of the whole People of God and their mission to be "light for the world."

James McGilvray is right in holding that "our life-style is the one factor which exercises the most decisive influence on our health." Hence, the Church's healing ministry obliges her to educate believers in this respect for the sake of health, wholeness, and salvation.

A healthy life-style — good nutrition, proper rest, balance between work and leisure, meaningful use of leisure time, physical exercise, refreshing contact with nature, development of a sense of beauty, and all such matters — can be learned from competent representatives of the various professions: physicians, therapists, dieticians, and others. But even more important are the many dimensions and aspects which faith helps us to uncover. Most vital is the development of the contemplative dimension of our existence. Through faith and contemplation we learn to discern between real and artificial needs and to acquire a taste for simplicity and thus gain internal and external freedom. We are freed from greed and desire for power, from useless worries, and so become open to joy in the Lord. Our freedom is a result of our surrender to the Holy Spirit who teaches us the liberating and healing power of love of God and neighbor, as well as purity of heart in all our relationships. An all-pervading spirit of thankfulness for the gifts of creation and redemption will motivate us to keep the earth habitable and attractive, to care for a healthy and beautiful environment.

As Christians, we should not care excessively for our own health, important as it is, but our life-style still must respond to our mission to be healers for others. Belief in Christ's sacrifice and a recognition of his being One-of-us, the Servant of all, give us clear direction and motivation for the right kind of living. The life-style of believers, particularly of those who are fully aware of their noble mission to share the Good News and to heal the sick, has to be convincing and attractive for all intelligent people.

Healing our own diseases

Since the invitation to be the first lecturer on the ''healing course'' established in remembrance of Blessed Peter Donders, the leper priest, was the treasured occasion for me to engage in deeper reflections about the blending of evangelization and healing, it seems appropriate to conclude with a thought on healing leprosy, both in others who have the actual disease and in ourselves who have the ''mental'' disease.

The healing love of Jesus for the lepers, his nearness to them, is a striking feature of Christ's revealing and healing presence. A grateful memory for this part of the Gospel message impels Christ's disciples and messengers to do whatever is in their power to heal humankind from this terrible disease and its devastating consequences, particularly now when this is actually possible. Medicine has given us the necessary key for fighting leprosy successfully. We are now asked whether, as Christians, we will use the keys which Christ has given us — healing love, generosity of commitment, and the spirit of sacrifice — to eradicate it completely.

Much has to be done. We know that it does not suffice to provide the relatively inexpensive medications and to detect contaminated persons in time to offer effective treatment. There is need to provide an all-embracing healthy environment and a healthy diet, especially for the children and all who are exposed to contamination. In the effort to fight leprosy, we face all the problems of the Third World: wholistic development, healthy socioeconomic and international relationships, personal cooperation, and promotion of co-responsibility on all levels.

The crusade against leprosy should be conducted in the spirit of the "wounded healer." As we open our hearts to the pitiful situation of the lepers, we should also open our eyes to our no less pitiable "leprosies": our dependence on artificially created needs, our numerous addictions, our greed which devours a vastly disproportionate share of the world's riches, our materialistic ideologies. All these and other "mental" leprosies carry the risk of a gradually induced spiritual vacuum, an existential emptiness that can cause a thousand evils.

The crusade to totally eliminate leprosy would take a decade or perhaps a few decades. It should go hand in hand with consciousness-raising about the greater evils which threaten humanity: the lust for power and possession, violence, war, enmity, the loss of the serenity provided by a simple life-style. Pictures which show the shocking ravages of leprosy should be weighed against the not less shocking results of alcoholism, drug addiction, terrorism, which are symptoms of our sick culture.

Our generous contributions to eliminate leprosy can very well come from what we gain by freeing ourselves for a simple life-style in eating, drinking, housing, traveling, and so on. Let us no longer look for what more we might need but, rather, for the many things which we could well renounce.

Take one example: if all our priests and religious would renounce the use of tobacco, avoid overeating, give up hard liquor, and contribute all they thus save for the healing of leprosy, how many forces would be set free for the joy of the Lord, the proclamation of the Good News, and for healing! How many healthier years could be added to the lives of priests and religious who are so badly needed! While the results would be marvelous for the lepers of the world, they would be even greater for so many threatened by alcoholism and drug addiction and for the smokers who are asking for lung cancers. Those who have not yet succeeded in freeing themselves from their addictions can find attractive patterns and strong motivations from those who have.

Here is a specific of what I mean. A certain priest told me this story. He was a zealous person who happened to be addicted to cigarette smoking. A good young man had consulted him on how to overcome a habit of frequent masturbation. In a moment of generosity the priest said to the young man: "I, too, have a bad habit — that of smoking. So, to help you, I promise to stop smoking right now. You pray for me to be able to fulfill my promise, and I will pray for you." The "miracle" happened; each was healed from his habit.

Our model of the "wounded healer" implies solidarity, mutual dependence. In our generous action for the elimination of leprosy, we should implore the lepers all over the world to pray for us that our society may become fully aware of its dangerous and contagious diseases and find strength to overcome them: diseases like wastefulness, greed, exploitation, collective egotism, air and water pollution, violence, injustice to poor countries and the poor in our own countries, polluted consciences brought on by a sick culture.

The liberation of humankind from actual and "mental" leprosy as well as similar evils is humanly possible; but it cannot be done without mustering our inner resources. Our effort to heal lepers and all those who are threatened by contamination will stimulate our energies, sharpen our consciences, and strengthen our efforts to free ourselves and our culture from the diseases of our own time and place, especially from violence, the arms race, and all forms of terrorism.

And all this will take place because we, like the apostles, will continue to proclaim everywhere the Good News which will always be accompanied by the signs of healing (see Luke 16:20).

SUGGESTED READINGS

Berne, Eric, *Games People Play*
Cuddihy, J. Murray, *The Ordeal of Civility*
Frankl, Viktor E., *The Doctor and the Soul: From Psychotherapy to Logotherapy*
Häring, Bernard, *Free and Faithful in Christ*
Jeremias, J., *New Testament Theology*
John Paul II, *Salvifici Doloris*
Jung, Carl G., *Analytical Psychology*
Kelsey, Morton, *Healing and Christianity*
Kovel, J., *A Complete Guide to Therapy*
Kubler-Ross, E., *Death: The Final Stage of Growth*
Linn, D. & M., *Healing Life's Hurts*
Marvin, E. W., *Planning for the Elderly*
May, Rollo, *Man's Search for Himself*
McGilvray, J., *The Quest for Health and Holiness*
McNutt, F., *Healing*
_____, *The Power to Heal*
Menninger, Karl, *Whatever Became of Sin?*
Minear, P. S., *To Heal and to Reveal*
Parkhurst, G., *Healing and Wholeness*
Sanford, Agnes, *The Healing Light*
Sanford, John, *Ministry Burnout*
Stanley, D. M., *Salvation and Healing*
Stoddard, Sandol, *The Hospice Movement*
Tyrrell, Bernard, *Christotherapy: Healing Through Enlightenment*

Other helpful books by the same author, Father Bernard Häring

IN PURSUIT OF HOLINESS
A simple yet profound book that offers wisdom, spiritual direction, and ways to discover "holiness" in yourself and others. $2.95

DARE TO BE CHRISTIAN
A beautiful invitation to see Christ by seeing the problems of others and to reach Christ by reaching out to others. $4.25

HEART OF JESUS: Symbol of Redeeming Love
Thirty inspiring meditations on the Sacred Heart plus a short history that clearly shows this devotion is more than pious sentimentality. It is based on the Bible and tradition. $4.25

A "Christians Anonymous" program that offers 12 steps to Christian growth!

BECOMING A NEW PERSON
by Philip St. Romain
These practical steps will help any Christian who wants to overcome the stumbling block of selfishness on the way to a more fulfilling future. The reader is invited to look inside for strength — out to others — and beyond to God. $2.95

Order from your local bookstore or write to:
Liguori Publications, Box 060, Liguori, Missouri 63057.
*(Please add 50¢ for postage and handling for first
item ordered and 25¢ for each additional item.)*